Written from the
the pages, Decepti
journey toward a more vital, vibrant faith. Deb's story reveals how painful the detection of deception over a long period of time can be to those who have a difficult time coping with what they have learned and dealing with the fact that someone close to them has betrayed their trust. Yet, she opens her heart to herself, to God, to life - a masterpiece of Job 22:21-30.

Eddy Laird
Associate Professor of Education
McDaniel College

This is a book about power. The power of secrets, the power of self-doubt, the power of loneliness, the power of the abuse of trust and authority, the power of shame. But it is about more than those things. Deb Myers has written a book that describes the power of forgiveness, both of self and others. She also writes about the power of exposing those dark places in our lives to the light, thereby giving ourselves over to the light. She writes about the power of honesty and moving forward into a better story. She has written a book about the power of the hunger to be transformed, and then what it means to actually experience transformation. Deb's is a quiet power, but it is power. Her story is the power of a woman who took a long road to wholeness, but exhibits gratitude for both the wholeness and the road that led her to it. Whatever your journey has been, wherever you may find yourself on your own road, I believe you will find Deb's story to be something that gives you renewed hope and energy to continue the journey.

Jerry Redman
Managing Senior Partner
Second Life of Chattanooga
Chattanooga, Tennessee

In a memoir intrinsically interwoven with glimpses of life as a Deaf child of Deaf parents, Deb Myers gives us a straightforward and honest look into the mind, heart and emotions of herself as a teen who cherished a special relationship with a teacher she trusted – a relationship that turned sexual. This moving narrative takes us through her teen years, her college years and her adult years and the deeply heartbreaking struggles along the way – largely because she thought the relationship was her fault. Deception is an emotional and sensitive portrayal of the effects of sexual abuse and the road to healing with the help of her therapist, her husband and her love for Christ. It is a book that gives a voice to abused women and their struggles and a book that helps those who have not been abused gain an understanding of why abused children and people may blame themselves. It is also a book of healing and hope. It is truly a book you will not put down.

Amy Gregurich Lindley
Former board member of Deaf Abused Women's Network (DAWN)

A powerful true story of betrayal, abuse and the long healing journey back to hope. A simple writing style so raw that I could not put it down. Society faces teacher-student abuse in epidemic proportions today. Deb's honesty is astounding as she delves into the past. She ultimately finds faith and love that is uplifting. Many thanks to the author for sharing her true story that others may be helped.

Anna L. Peterson, LCSW -C

This amazing read leads you on a journey of survival—from confusion, shame and self-blame to Deb finally reclaiming her life.

Tiffany S. Williams
Executive Director
Abused Deaf Women Advocacy Services (ADWAS)

deception

deception

A Deaf Girl's Journey Through Trust, Betrayal, Abuse, and Redemption

Deb Myers

LIFE SENTENCE
Publishing, LLC

www.lifesentencepublishing.com

Like us on Facebook

deception – Deb Myers

Copyright © 2014

Printed in the United States of America

First edition published 2013

LIFE SENTENCE Publishing books are available at discounted prices for ministries and other outreach.

Find out more by contacting us at info@lifesentencepublishing.com

LIFE SENTENCE Publishing and its logo are trademarks of

LIFE SENTENCE Publishing, LLC
P.O. Box 652
Abbotsford, WI 54405

Paperback ISBN: 978-1-62245-151-7

Ebook ISBN: 978-1-62245-152-4

10 9 8 7 6 5 4 3 2 1

This book is available from www.amazon.com, Barnes & Noble, and your local Christian bookstore.

Cover Design: Amber Burger

Editor: Joan O'Brien

Contents

Foreword

"The coexistence of Friendship and Eros may . . .
help some moderns to realise [sic]
that Friendship is in reality a love,
and even as great a love as Eros."
(C. S. Lewis, The Four Loves, p. 99)

Certainly, C. S. Lewis is not equating friendship love as erotic love between teenagers and adults. However, a love that begins as friendship, and grows into lifelong marriage commitment, is often the best foundation for a satisfactory sexual relationship. But Lewis does have a point.

Sometimes there is confusion as to which form of love is expressed between humans. Those nearing adulthood can mistake heightened activity in the brain for adult feelings of love. Love expressions by teenagers are not the same as mature adult expressions of love. That being the case, the addition of physical or sexual relations between an adult and a teenager confuses the hearts of both, and improperly connects unstable emotions and preoccupies the minds. Pleasure to an adult is dissimilar to pleasure to a teenager, especially when the heart is the motivating factor. For "out of the heart . . . come evil thoughts, sexual immorality . . . adultery . . ." (ESV Mark 7:21)

Teenagers do not make adult distinctions between physical pleasure and emotional stability. Teenagers are crush-oriented and mature adults tend toward unconditional love. However, teenagers and adults who connect emotionally over time, or begin sharing their personal problems with each other in private, risk blurring what is actually taking place. As a result, physical relations may be right around the corner.

Trusted adults making profound connections with teenagers, have not changed much over the years. It is just that in today's world of ubiquitous sexuality and rising sexual predation – nurtured by adults and teenagers online – we find newer and easier fertile ground. This new ground is where the seeds of relationship ruination may take root.

Compounding matters of the heart is the human brain, which because of age, maturity, and a host of other biological and choice-oriented factors, involves a vast range emotions. Teenage brains are not adult brains. Teenage romantic affections naturally run amuck, let alone when adults are the targets. An adult entrusted with authority over a teenager, who finds his or her emotions connecting deeply with those of a teenager, must seek advice on how to handle and even diffuse these emotions.

Neuroscientists today are discovering new and wonderful things about the brains of teenagers, and the differences that exist between their brains and adult brains. One thing most adults already know is that teenagers are highly emotional, and that these emotions seem larger-than-life. The reasons for these heightened states of emotions are because of the flow of neuro-chemicals and neuro-connections in the teenagers' brains, all of which characterizes lesser-mature brains. Teenagers naturally draw toward friends and strive for acceptance by their peers – often defending themselves and their choices to extremes, in the process.

Lewis had it right about friendship love. However, teenagers also seek acceptance by those in authority over them. Whether teachers, coaches, or administrators, sometimes it is easy to misconstrue teenage attention as teenage romantic affection. Therefore, if left uncorrected, the adult and teenager run the risk of an improper emotional connection – the likes of which may result in something more physical because of personal desires for acceptance.

Classroom teachers must especially be on guard. Their environment brings with it a natural social packaging, as well as heightened emotional states. A problem begins to arise when teachers allow themselves to think students' very "fired-up" teenage brains are fully-developed emotionally and can handle adult-relationships.

Matters of the heart and brain are as tricky as they are complicated. Deb Myers has written this personal memoir titled *Deception*, in which she chronicles a period in her own life where she crosses into an inappropriate teacher-student relationship. As you will see in her journal entries, emotional connections result from a series of choices. At first, expressions of empathy draw the two together. Over time, the teacher becomes emotionally significant in Myers' life.

As a teenage student, Myers willingly returns these affections, and validation by her teacher makes her feel good. However, does she really know she is actually the victim? Most teenagers do not. This bond between teacher and student eventually finds its way into a physical and sexual relationship. This should serve as a warning: Emotional bonds between adults and teenagers that result in sex, produce their own forms of bondage, as the reader will come to understand.

Every day, there are appropriate and inappropriate relationships that take place between teachers and their students. In terms of the latter, no distinction is made – whether we speak of Christian schools, various private and parochial schools, or public schools. The law makes no such distinction either, as to faith or tenet, or educational philosophy when a crime is committed. The reality is, sexual predators and sex-offenders are of both genders, of all ages, and come from all backgrounds and professions.

It is true that humans are sexual creatures that seek friendly affections and attention from others. Yet, there must be boundaries. The classroom is no exception to this rule. Myers illustrates clearly that teenagers making adult-like choices are not the same as adults making choices. Both are self-serving, but there are vast differences. God is working and Myers discovers that the Almighty "creates clean hearts, and renews right spirits" within us (Psalm 51:10). When it comes to teachers having sexual relationships with students, we can be certain that the teachers are certainly not the victims in these situations.

There are many environments where adults and teenagers work in close proximity. Teenage students and their teachers are never to be encouraged to cross boundaries with each other. However, these boundaries must first be set. This can especially difficult when the teacher is close in age to his or her students, or when particular relational nuances add special considerations in communicating matters of the heart.

Teachers are naturally given toward compassion and moral purpose. This is confirmed by Michael Fullan, in his book *Change Forces*, where he writes, if we scratch below the surface of a good teacher, "we would find moral purpose." Teachers and students involving themselves in inappropriate relationships compromise both the student's moral development and diminish the teacher's entrusted moral high road.

Ernest J. Zarra, III, Ph.D.
Author, *Teacher-Student Relationships:*
Crossing Into the Emotional,
Physical, and Sexual Realms
February 14, 2014, Valentine's Day

Acknowledgements

Holy Spirit, you nudged me to write. I do not yet know the outcome, but I trust that my story will help someone. Thank you for using my book to reach others in whatever ways you desire.

Peter, my devoted and much-loved husband of 24 years, this book wouldn't have been possible without your love, support, and encouragement. Thank you for always being there 24/7.

Savannah, Seth, Summer, I was awestruck by your non-judgmental reaction when I shared my past with you. Thank you for allowing me to share my life with the readers.

Sumangal and Shantou, you don't yet fully understand what my book is about. Thank you for your patience as I sat glued to the computer all day long, writing.

Pete Rothenhoefer, you recognized my style of writing with encouraging words. Thank you for the time you gave me.

Dan Rotach, Peb Rock, Jeremiah Kelly, and Jenn Dorsch, thank you for making yourselves available to read my manuscript in its early stages.

Kate Etue, thank you for your invaluable help in editing the original manuscript.

Anna Peterson, you came along at the right time. Thank you for caring enough to speak the truth.

Life Sentence Publishing, thank you for believing that my book has a place on bookshelves.

Prologue

June 1989

I glanced over my shoulder to make sure no cars were approaching before stepping into the street to open our mailbox. I quickly spotted two cream-colored envelopes in the bundle of mail. On the upper right corner were the twenty-five cent stamps I had personally licked and stuck on. I knew without opening it that the RSVP card inside had raised flowers printed on the upper left corner. The leaves around the flowers extended down to the bottom left corner. The card was simple in its design – just the way I wanted.

I looked at the return addresses to see who had responded. The minute I saw his name, my stomach became queasy. Forgetting I was only two feet from the road, with cars passing by every few minutes, I stood there, unable to move. It was as if every living thing around me held its breath.

Why does his name continue to have such an effect on me? I closed my eyes and shook my head, not wanting to re-read the chapter I had already finished. *Will it be a Yes or Regrets?* After several seconds, I sighed, realizing I'd better return to the house or else Mom would probably wonder what was the matter with me.

Mom was sitting in her favorite spot on the couch in the living room, her eyes glued to *Days of Our Lives* on the television when I opened the front door. As soon as I stepped into the living room, she glanced at me. Seeing that I had picked up the mail, she raised her eyebrows, questioning. Without a word, I knew what she was asking: "How many people have responded?"

"Two," I answered, walking across the living room into the dining room, not wanting to talk further.

Fortunately, Mom's show was captivating, which meant that she would be glued to her seat for the next forty minutes. I pulled out a dining room chair from the table and sat down. It took me several minutes before I was able to open the envelope. Slowly, I pulled out the RSVP-before-July-15-1989 card and stared long and hard at his familiar handwriting:

He is coming.

Why did I invite him? Why couldn't he just say he wasn't able to attend? Not that I really needed answers. I did not have much choice. I had to invite him. He probably felt he had to come. Otherwise, it would raise too many questions.

Chapter 1

1977

From a very young age I could tell I was the envy of Mom and Dad's friends. Not because I was born with natural beauty or with a special talent, but because I was born Deaf. My being Deaf meant Mom and Dad would be able to pass on their Deaf culture to me – the next generation. It also meant convenience, in a way, being able to converse with their child in their natural language – American Sign Language (ASL).

I was also Mom and Dad's friends' next generation. Along with my Deaf peers, I represented the future of Deaf people. I could relate with their experiences. We shared similar upbringings – life at a residential school. We understood each other's frustrations in how we were treated in the hearing world. We discussed happenings within the Deaf community and shared Deaf jokes. Among Mom and Dad's circle of friends, I was the only child who was Deaf. Because of that, I often hung around them rather than with their children or my siblings.

At our house, Mom and her female friends sat around the dining room table, catching up on each other's lives. Of course, there was gossip. They discussed *Days of Our Lives* and *All My Children*. Never mind that in those days, TV shows were not closed-captioned. Their conversations were made all the more lively by the fact that they would deduce what had happened, and then, when they got together, they would compare notes about their assumptions.

The men either stood outside or in the kitchen, discussing various topics – work, sports, and the news. I would shift between the two groups, although I preferred the men. They were more fun to be around, and we teased each other a lot.

One Friday night, I tried out the latest joke on Terry, one of Dad's friends. I held a dessert plate in my left hand, and with my right hand, I passed on an identical plate to him. Then, I gave instructions: "Keep your eyes on my face the whole time and copy exactly what I do. Okay? I'll see how well you can copy me."

Terry laughed and looked at everyone forming a circle to see the show. "She thinks she's smart. This shouldn't be too hard," Terry said.

"Okay, are you ready?" I challenged him.

"I'm ready," he responded with confidence.

With the plate still in my left hand, my right finger circled the bottom of the plate. I lifted my finger to my chin and touched it there. Terry copied my exact movement; so far, so good. My finger returned to the bottom of the plate, and I repeated myself, touching a different place on my face. This went on for several minutes. When I was satisfied with what I saw, I held out my right hand and asked for his plate.

"You did great," I told Terry. "I'm finished."

Looking at everyone, I asked: "What do you think?"

Everyone laughed and commented: "You'd better look in the mirror!" "She's smart!" "Wish I had camera!"

With everyone trailing behind, Terry walked into our bathroom and looked in the mirror. His face was covered with black marks. Prior to pulling the prank, I had burned the bottom of his plate with a match, creating black soot.

"You! You got me this time," he said, wrapping his arm around my shoulder for an affectionate hug. "I'll get you back."

"I'll see if you can," I said, laughing.

I enjoyed being the center of attention. It would be several years until I realized what was missing in our house – Mom and Dad's affection.

Chapter 2

Early years with Mom

When I was young, I looked up to Mom. In my eyes, she was a superwoman. I had close friends at school, but when I was home on weekends, Mom was my playmate and best friend.

As I'd fill her in on my time away during the week, Mom loved to reminisce about her life at the Pennsylvania School for the Deaf (PSD) where she grew up. She would tell me how each time when she'd return to campus her dormitory counselor would force her head into a sink, pour terrible-smelling medicated shampoo onto her hair, and scrub roughly. The counselor would then wrap her head tightly in a towel. This was to ensure that all potential lice eggs would be killed. All this happened even though Mom claimed she did not have lice. To make matters worse, not every student had to go through this humiliating procedure.

She shared how the teachers would whip her hands with a ruler when she was caught signing in the classroom or between classes. The teachers would drill her in making a specific sound through her nose, learning to enunciate. When Mom was not able to make the sound correctly, the teacher would pinch and jerk her nose, which would sometimes result in a nose-bleed. And she told how her dorm counselor would inspect her bed in the mornings before school. If her sheets were one inch longer on one side than on the other, the counselor would strip the sheets off the bed and force Mom to remake her bed. No matter how many times Mom told me her stories, I never grew tired of hearing them. Her experience was so unlike mine.

Mom was the youngest of fourteen siblings. (Her mom stopped having children after she miscarried her fifteenth child.) Despite the fact that she was the youngest, Mom was the first to graduate from high school. "If I had not attended PSD, I would have quit just like my sisters and brothers to help out with farm work," she said thankfully. She had lived at the residential school her entire life, Kindergarten through her senior year in high school. Her trips home were limited to Christmas break and summer.

I envied Mom. Her farm tales sounded fun. While milking the cow, she would sneak in a drink directly from the udder. She described how the chickens were killed: "My father would hold them by their necks and cut off their heads. Then, they would run around flapping with blood spurting out of their necks."

"They were still alive?" My young mind had difficulty imagining such a scene.

Mom was not afraid of anything. A snake? Not a problem. She'd split it in half with a shovel. Bat? She'd grab a broom, open the bedroom window, and lure the bat out of the closet. Huge hairy spider? She smashed it with a napkin. Mouse? After Mom released the dead mouse from the trap, she would hold it by its tail and chase us to test our reactions. I never questioned her ability to protect my siblings and me from nature's harm.

Everything my siblings and I did, Mom insisted she was capable of doing the same, and even better than us. She could run as fast as we could. She could beat us in an arm-wrestling contest. She could twirl a Hula-Hoop without letting it fall. She could ride a bike without holding the handlebars – that is, until the day she took a bad fall and learned her lesson. Not to mention all the board games she would win. She was no merciful player either. If Mom lost, it meant one of us had cheated. If we denied it, she would demand a rematch.

My friends thought Mom was cool. She participated in our games, helping us find good places to hide during hide and seek. At night, when we were ready to sleep, Mom would sneak outside to spook us through the bedroom window, scaring us out of our skin. Mom would show off her strength by flexing her muscles; my friends' jaws would drop seeing how strong Mom was.

You could tell how hard a worker Mom was just by looking at her hands. They were not smooth and silky. Every spring, she and Dad planted vegetables – corn, potatoes, lima beans, string beans, peas, zucchini, squash, tomatoes, cucumbers, green peppers, and onions. We also grew strawberries, watermelons, and cantaloupes. After harvesting, Mom would either freeze or can the summer bounty.

Indeed, Mom was a superwoman. She was the one who could do it all. She was our housekeeper. She was our cook. She was our hairdresser and barber. She was our seamstress. She was our banker. And so much more.

Unfortunately, what Mom couldn't do were the things I needed most from her.

Chapter 3

1978

My younger sister Connie walked into our bedroom and burst into tears.

"What's the matter?" I asked.

"I don't want to call," she sobbed. No explanation was needed. Mom or Dad had asked her to make a phone call. To whom, I wasn't sure. It could be that Dad wanted her to call someone regarding a letter or a bill that he had received. It could be that Mom wanted her to schedule a doctor's appointment. It could be that Dad wanted her to relay a message to someone.

"Don't," I commanded.

"Mom will be so mad."

"I'll go to talk to her now," I said.

"No," she pleaded. "Please don't. She will get angry."

I ignored Connie and stormed out of our bedroom. I had assumed the role of peacemaker, settling disputes or misunderstandings between Mom and Dad and my siblings (and at times people outside home). I was overprotective of my siblings, especially Connie, because she was next in line. Unfortunately, I was not around them much. I lived at the Maryland School for the Deaf (MSD), and I was home only on weekends, forty-nine hours to be exact, not including holidays and summers.

When I was away at school, all the responsibilities that would have normally been mine fell on her shoulders. To make matters worse, she was hearing, which meant she had one added responsibility that I did not have to deal with – interpreting.

It had happened one time too many and I was fed up. Why couldn't Mom or Dad understand? Connie was only a child.

"Who did you want Connie to call?" I asked.

Mom looked at Dad. "See. Connie always tattle-tells. Connie does not want to help us. You all never want to help," she accused me.

"Not true!" I argued back. I listed all the times we had helped her. But it didn't matter. Mom wouldn't listen. As always, Dad just stood there, speechless. He was never much help.

"Sue is very lucky! Very, very lucky," Mom said. "Missy always helps Sue and Bill. She never complains. Same with Dawn. She always helps her parents. Right?" Mom looked at Dad.

Dad said nothing.

Mom continued: "Connie always complains. Complains!"

"Connie is so young," I tried to make Mom and Dad understand. "Some of the words are hard for her to interpret. She does not know those people, so she does not feel comfortable talking. Why don't you ask Grandma or Harold to help you?"

"Not Grandma's business to know who we want to call. If I ask Harold, he would wonder why I don't ask my *own* children. Connie can call. I know she can do it."

"You just don't understand." The minute I said it, I wished I hadn't.

"You think I'm stupid?" Mom glanced at Dad. "See. She thinks I'm stupid! I knew it."

Dad finally tried to intervene. He looked at both of us and said, "Just forget it." As if that would resolve our problem.

"I never said the word *stupid*. I did not say that! You added that word yourself. I said you don't understand why Connie does not want to call," I tried to explain. "Some words are hard for her. Better to ask Grandma or someone else so that there's no misunderstanding."

"Ha! Connie knows the words. You all don't help because

you don't love me. I know it," Mom reasoned. She added, "If I die, you wouldn't care."

"Not true! Please don't say that," I begged. This kind of talk scared me, but at the same time it never made me stop arguing with her. She had threatened numerous times in the past that she would go into the garage, get in the car, start the motor, and let it run so that the carbon monoxide would kill her.

I let out an exasperated sigh as I stormed out of the room – another day and another bungled attempt at expressing our thoughts and feelings.

Chapter 4

Early years with Dad

*P*eople often tell me that I looked like Dad. We have similar features, except for our ears – his are quite large. I also inherited his laid-back personality. We both grew up attending the same residential school – MSD. Dad graduated with the class of 1959, and I would in 1985. We even shared the same teacher, Ms. Mooring, in elementary school; she seemed so old to me, wrinkles and all. She liked to tell me how she always had to tie Dad's shoes when his laces came loose.

Everyone in our hometown seemed to know Dad. He was not famous, mind you, but everywhere we went, there'd be at least one person walking over to shake Dad's hand. The person extending his hand would begin to talk, and Dad would smile and nod as if he understood everything. I would nudge Dad and say, "You don't even know what he said." As soon as the person stopped talking and left, Dad would begin reminiscing about how he'd known that person in the old days. You see, Williamsport was a small town of less than 1,800 people. My dad grew up here. My grandfather graduated from Williamsport High School and was known as a great athlete. My paternal great-grandfather was well-known in the community; he was a county superintendent of roads, and served as a board member of our local bank. Several of my relatives still lived in the area. Because Dad was Deaf, I suppose, he was someone people didn't easily forget.

Dad had a strong work ethic. Right after his graduation, he was employed by Moller Organ – a factory that manufactured handcrafted pipe organs. His work was unique – he was Deaf, and yet, he was a part of the company that built pipe organs which produced beautiful sounds in churches all over the world. His work required sharp eyes and precise measurement, and he was proud of his contribution to organ-making.

Dad was a friend to all – young and old, hearing and Deaf, uneducated and educated. We knew several Deaf elderly people who did not have driver's licenses, and Dad would gladly take them places – the annual summer Deaf picnic in Boonsboro, MSD reunion gatherings, and other Deaf-related events. I loved to tag along, and when I received my license, I also volunteered to take our older friends for their medicine, grocery shopping, or on errands.

Dad was proud of his good deeds and liked to tell me how the "world" couldn't manage without him. How he had taught his friends to play baseball. How his co-workers had depended on him to cover their duties at work, yet no one could cover Dad's station. How he was the first among his high school classmates to purchase a car with his own money and would chauffeur his friends around town after graduation because they didn't have cars.

Traditions were very important to Dad. We ate turkey or ham four times a year – Thanksgiving, Christmas, Easter, and on his birthday. He expected the same dishes to be served at each of those special occasions. And speaking of food, supper was served every afternoon at 4:30 p.m. sharp. He was never home late from work, always arriving between 4:21 and 4:23 p.m. He would put his black lunch box on the kitchen counter and wash his face and hands in the bathroom before sitting in his usual place at the table.

Dad was a huge fan of the Baltimore Orioles, the University of Maryland basketball, and the Washington Redskins. My Sundays – before returning to school – were spent sitting in front of the TV with him. He was forever telling me trivia about the players, and I even learned the players by their names. Dad rarely became angry, but if a referee made a lousy call or a player made a stupid mistake, we'd see his temper flare. But his anger was never directed toward us kids. He never laid a finger on us. In fact, if Mom sent us to our rooms, he'd let us out as soon as she left the house.

Dad gave me what he could, the only way he knew how. Yet his soft heart and good nature couldn't give me what I needed most. I needed a "daddy." But that just couldn't be.

Chapter 5

May 1989

Grandma and I stepped into a small florist located several miles from our home. I had passed this storefront growing up but had never been inside the shop. As I stood next to Grandma, my eyes scanned the flowers on display. Grandma proudly introduced me to the florist, resting her hand on my arm. I smiled as they chatted. Throughout the conversation, Grandma kept patting my arm. I had no idea what was being exchanged, although I knew they were talking about me. The florist kept stealing glances at me and smiling.

Grandma was probably telling the florist that I had recently graduated from Gallaudet and that I was now working as a psycho-social counselor in Baltimore, with Deaf and chronically mentally ill clients. I knew she was proud of me and my accomplishments.

I grew up next door to my grandma. I loved her dearly, despite her inability to communicate with me in depth. She knew some basic signs, but beyond that, we depended on paper and pen. I knew she loved me. Every time I walked into the house, she would drop everything she was doing to greet me.

"May I see the flowers?" I gestured, Grandma relaying the message. The florist immediately put on her professional front and escorted me to a tiny table that held two books. After I settled into one of the chairs, she resumed her conversation with Grandma.

It didn't take long before I fell in love with the most beautiful bouquet – a bright, colorful mixture of delphinium, daisies,

stargazer lilies, statices, and freesia. Small green leaves comple-
mented the arrangement.

"Oh, pretty," Grandma agreed.

I looked at Grandma with a thankful heart as the florist
filled out our order. Grandma had offered to pay for the flowers.
And, bless the florist's heart, she gave us a discount. It helped
that Grandma and the florist had a long-standing relationship;
they had worked together for many years. As a member of Zion
Evangelical Lutheran Church, Grandma was responsible for
setting up flowers in the sanctuary.

Actually, she had a lot of responsibilities at the church. She
even had her own key. I would often accompany Grandma to
church on Saturdays while she made sure everything was ready
for the Sunday service. I would just roam around, looking at
nothing in particular, not paying attention to what she was
doing. But I knew God played an important role in Grandma's
life – beyond her service to her church. At home, I would find
her sitting in her favorite armchair in the living room, with
the Bible open on her lap, reading. Though she never talked to
me about it, her actions displayed her deep love and reverence
for our Lord.

Chapter 6

Fall 1980

*I*t was a typical Friday when our bus pulled into the high school parking lot. I scanned the lot and spotted Grandma's car. Mom would pick me up some Fridays, but mostly it was Grandma.

When the bus rolled to a stop, ten or so of us got up and stood in a line. We moved slowly as each person, elementary through high school, stepped off the bus. We waited patiently as the bus driver hopped out, walked to the rear side of the bus, and opened the compartment containing everyone's belongings.

During my elementary years, I had a black suitcase; the tag attached spelled my full name. Every piece of clothing packed into the suitcase had my name sewn in it. As I got older, I outgrew the small black suitcase, and my clothes were no longer identified with my name.

This afternoon I had my blue suitcase in hand, and I walked across the parking lot to Grandma's car, opened the back door, tossed the suitcase on the seat, and flopped into the front seat. Not much was exchanged between us; our conversation would have to wait until sometime during the weekend, when we would sit by her tiny table in the kitchen with paper and pen, writing back and forth.

When I arrived home, I opened the front door and went straight to my room to change into comfortable clothes, as always. I also checked, out of habit, to ensure that my diary was in its place under my winter sweaters on the shelf Dad had built inside my closet. This time my diary was not underneath the first sweater. Perhaps I had put it between the second and third. Not there, either. My heart began to race as I groped everywhere – underneath, inside the sweaters, and behind the pile of sweaters.

I backed out of the closet, trying to focus. Had I hid it elsewhere? I checked every possible hiding place – inside my drawer, under the mattress, and under the chair cushion. Empty-handed, I sat down on my bed, a sickening feeling building inside me.

It's not that I had written something bad or secretive. I hid it because I shared a room with my sister, Connie, and I didn't want her to come across the diary. She was two years younger than I was, and I didn't want her to read about Randy kissing me.

Had Connie taken the diary? Had she read it? Had Mom? How would I ever find out without asking?

Chapter 7

Same day

Mom appeared in the doorway of my bedroom. After few seconds of silence, she finally asked: "How was school?"

"Fine."

Mom looked at me, nodding. She wore an expression I knew too well. She was holding something back.

"What's the matter?" I asked.

"I found out." It was her passive aggressive behavior that I had grown to loathe.

"Found out what?" I asked, hoping it had nothing to do with my diary.

"You tell me."

"What are you talking about?"

"Now I see. You've been lying," Mom accused.

"Lying about what?" I had no idea what she was talking about.

"You had sex with Randy."

I was stunned. Then I began to feel angry. How could she read my diary? It was mine.

"I did not," I protested. "You misunderstood."

"You think I'm stupid?"

"I'm telling you the truth. Honestly, I did not."

"So, you have been lying. Now I know what you have been up to."

"Please," I begged. "Give back my diary. Show me where I said I had sex."

"It's too late."

"What do you mean?"

"I threw it away."

"No, you did not!" I knew she was lying. "Please give it back," I begged. She had completely misunderstood my writing.

"I don't have it. I don't want to talk about it anymore."

Randy and I attended a camp earlier that summer. He was the first boy I had kissed. We weren't boyfriend and girlfriend, but we had experimented with kissing. At the camp, the two of us had wandered off to the woods...

"Please give it back. We will read it together and I will explain what I mean."

"It's over." She walked away.

That was the end of our conversation. Why she was so upset, I had no clue. The topic of sex was not taboo in our house, except around my siblings. Growing up, I had often hung around Mom and Dad's friends, and I knew what sex was all about.

Sex was a fairly open topic. So what was upsetting Mom? I had not mentioned a single word about sex in my diary.

Over the next couple of weekends, when I was home, I would sneak into Mom and Dad's bedroom, looking for my diary. I checked every possible hiding place. But it was nowhere to be found.

Chapter 8

Fall 1980

*B*ridgetta and I exchanged our first secret when we were nine or ten years old.

Her secret? Well, I can't reveal it because I promised that I'd never tell.

My secret? As a nine-year-old, my written English was better than my mom's. In fact, I helped her compose letters and complete paperwork. When I received letters from Mom, Bridgetta and I would hide behind the big chair in the corner of our dormitory living room and read them together. She was the only one who could understand the diary incident.

"Did you know that God forbids sex until after marriage?" Bridgetta asked.

"Really? Why?" I'd never heard such a thing.

At that point in my life, I knew very little about God. Mom and Dad didn't attend church regularly, and when we did go, I had to sit with them in the adult worship service; there were no Sunday school classes for Deaf kids. I once won a picture of Jesus at church, and I hung it on the wall of my bedroom. He was kneeling by a rock, praying. The two-inch golden frame had a small light on the top, and when I turned it on, Jesus glowed beautifully. I often looked at the picture, especially at night. It had a calming effect on me. But I knew very little of who this man was. I knew we shouldn't lie, cheat, or steal. And I learned a few Bible stories when a church invited some Deaf children to come to Vacation Bible School one summer – Adam and Eve, Noah's Ark, and David and Goliath. Other than those stories, though, I knew almost nothing. So I was surprised to hear God had a say about *sex*.

Bridgetta proceeded with her testimony – Adam and Eve had sinned, and all of us are sinners. Jesus had died for our sins, and He wanted us to live forever with Him in heaven. She explained that God wanted us to obey Him, and that if we didn't, we would be doomed to hell.

"Hell?"

I was scared. So I believed her. Why wouldn't I? Her parents were smarter than mine, and they taught her those things. Right there, I confessed my sins and invited Jesus into my heart.

Prior to this conversation, I had never known sex was a precious gift that God intended only for marriage. This knowledge stayed with me and I was determined to follow His command. Our discussion also sparked my interest in learning more about God and His Word.

Chapter 9

Spring 1981

At home for the weekend once again, I entered Mom and Dad's bedroom, carefully scanning. Which hiding places had I missed? It had been months, and I was still determined to find my diary. Whenever Mom would leave the house – to hang her clothes, work in the garden, or run errands – I would continue to search.

I didn't believe that Mom had thrown away the diary. Mom was not always honest. However, after our argument, this subject was never brought up again. Mom was very stubborn; once her mind was made up there was no room for discussion.

My eyes scanned every inch of the room, when I laid eyes on a framed picture of my maternal grandparents. Unlike Dad's mother, Grandma, who always kept her hair short and stylish, Mom's mother, Grandmother, tied her hair in a bun. It was thin and grayish, and when left loose, fell down to her waist. Whenever we visited, I would watch her brush her long hair. Then she would braid it. I was fascinated by the way she removed loose hair from her hairbrush and used it to secure her braid at the bottom. A rubber band was not needed. She wore tattered calf-length dresses with thick panty hose, often with runs. Grandfather wore faded overalls, which didn't always look clean. He chewed tobacco, spitting into an empty Yam can, which was left on the windowsill for everyone to see. They were much older than my dad's parents; Grandmother was forty-two when my mom was born.

The picture frame!

Could it be? My diary was written on composition paper, and there were only five or six pages. I quickly walked over to the window to spy Mom. I didn't have much time. She was almost done removing the clothes from the clothesline.

Hurriedly, I lifted the picture off the wall and slid the cardboard from behind the frame. And there I saw my handwriting. My diary. I quickly removed the papers, returned the cardboard to its place, and hung the picture where it belonged.

My plan was set. I walked into our bathroom and locked the door. Sitting down on the closed toilet lid, I read for the last time what I had written. I found the part where I had written about wandering off into the woods. Randy had pulled me down to the ground on top of him. We had only hugged and kissed. Mom had jumped to conclusions, thinking that Randy and I didn't have our clothes on. She didn't give me the opportunity to explain or to clarify.

I hated the thought of letting go of my diary, but I knew I had to destroy it. I turned on the water faucet, clicked on the exhaust fan, and lit the match, carefully burning each page, one by one, and watching the ashes go down the drain.

I never told Mom that I had found the diary. And if Mom knew, she never said anything.

Chapter 10

May 1989

I inspected the napkins that had arrived in the mail. Our names and the wedding date were correct. I was relieved. As soon as I saw the picture in one of the wedding-supply catalogs, I knew I had found the perfect design for our wedding.

"I've never seen such thing," Mom said. "For a wedding? It's unheard of."

I ignored her comments. She had assumed I would pick a more traditional design. The square-shaped napkin had a simple picture of a boy and a girl walking in the grass, holding hands. The little boy was dressed in a short sleeve t-shirt and blue jeans, and the girl, who was the same height, was dressed in overalls. The girl's right hand rested in her right rear pocket. Her straight, long hair fell down past her shoulder. Below the picture the napkin read: THIS DAY I WILL MARRY MY FRIEND.

I knew those attending the wedding would think the design was most fitting. For most of my life, I left my hair long and straight. And, I had practically lived in overalls during my high school years.

Yes, I'm going to marry and spend the rest of my life with my best friend. Besterest, as we often referred to each other – good, better, best, bester, besterest. Get it? There's no such word in the dictionary. But for us, it was perfect.

Chapter 11

Spring 1982

I noticed subtle differences between my parents and my friends' parents. At a young age, I didn't think too much about it. After all, my life at home was what I knew; I couldn't imagine it any other way. But as I grew older, and the more time I spent at my friends' houses, I began to envy their parents' hugs and kisses, or when they simply asked them interestedly about school. They would also ask me what I learned that week, what subject I liked best, and other things to get to know me better. My heart would race. I felt cornered, and I would be so glad when they would let me go. Yet, I pondered what it must be like to have parents who cared about you.

Unlike a typical teenager without a care in the world, I knew too much. I knew my Dad's income. I knew how much money my parents had in savings, or perhaps I should say how little. Mom would say to me, "Don't tell this to Connie or David, they are so young." The secrets had made me feel grown-up and important, but what a burden they had been. Knowing their finances, I made every effort to forego any unnecessary expenses. I never asked for brand-name clothing or shoes. Once or twice a year, when we traveled to visit my mom's parents, Mom and Dad would treat us at McDonald's; it was the only place we ever ate out. Everyone would order whatever they pleased. But not me. I always ordered the cheapest meal – a 49-cent hamburger and a cup of water.

It seemed as if my parents always needed help, and I made it my responsibility to ensure they understood anything that was being communicated to them. Sometimes I had no clue how to do or say what was needed – I was just a kid myself – but somehow, I managed. For example, when I was in elementary school, a classmate of mine had invited me to go home with her for the weekend. Mom had to write a permission note for me to change my regular plans, so I had her copy my writing: "I have Debbie's permission to spend the weekend…" Of course, she should have written: "Debbie has my permission…" Those times when I realized my mistakes were so embarrassing.

Though mature for my age, I was in other ways a typical teenager. I was a rather quiet and reserved girl, but once people knew me I was fun to be around. I was well liked by my peers and got along with everyone. My report cards would have made any parent proud. I was an obedient child, and I displayed a pleasant and positive attitude. My life at school was a happy one.

I had my first boyfriend at fourteen. I don't recall how or when David and I first became attracted to each other. I don't even remember our first kiss. The first picture I have of us together was in May 1981, just before my fourteenth birthday. The following year, my photo album was filled with pictures of him – and us.

David's upbringing was very different from mine. He came from a hearing family and was the younger of two. His family attended church every Sunday. He lived within a few miles of MSD and was a day student. In other words, unlike most of us, he did not sleep in the dorm. I would go over to his house sometimes on Sunday evenings when I arrived back at school after the weekend at home.

Our times together were fun. We teased each other a lot and laughed often. We both liked sports – he played football and basketball – and I was on the basketball and track teams. We would cheer for each other when we could. He even sneaked out of his class one afternoon so he could watch me run in the track meet. Later, when he got his driver's license, we would sometimes sneak off campus without permission and just drive around together.

He was someone I could talk to easily. He was comfortable expressing his emotions – I even saw him cry. I suppose he learned that from his mother. He once told me how she would cry when he was giving her a hard time. A mother who showed sorrow and expressed pain – that was something new to me.

Chapter 12

March 1983

*D*avid and I called each other often, especially on Sundays when we were not able to see each other. One Sunday in March, I called him from my dorm lobby:

David: Hi, Dave here. GA [This is a TTY code for Go Ahead.]

Me: Hi, darling! This is your darling. Hold Ok, I just turned the light on cuz it is dark here. Ha. Well, how was your afternoon? GA

David: Well, I practiced. It was good, then I got home and watched some basketball. I asked mom if I could see you, but she said no. I was disappointed, then I started on science homework. I really wanted to see you, but sorry – it's my fault. GA

Me: Don't blame yourself. It's not your fault. Are you done with your science homework? GA

David: No way. I did chapter 30. I have to do chapter 31, 32 qs, and I will finish it after I talk with my beautiful darling, who I miss very much already. Ha!

Me: Yeah, I miss you too, but it's your fault that we can't see each other now. Just kidding. Ok, when I arrived here I ate my supper, a sandwich, then I started to read a book until the girls arrived.

David: It was funny this morning because my pastor

came to me and shook my hand and signed good job. I thanked him. My parents said he and his wife enjoyed the [MSD Spring] play very much. Also, this morning Ina and her friend were here. Paula told all the people that she wanted to thank me for praying all three nights. She thinks that we will spread God's gospel to other people.

Well, you wrote me a note ... I forgot to tell you that I almost cried when you said you wanted to know more about God. I have always wanted to talk with you about God, but I don't know what to say. I'm sure God didn't like what we did last Friday night. I know this isn't as bad as sex, of course, and the Bible didn't say "thou cannot touch bodies," so I guess it was alright with God if I did that, but I know you did not feel comfortable. I'm sure God will get angry if we have sex before marriage, which of course we won't do. Do you have any suggestions about what we can do to share our relationship with God? He'll be happy to be part of us. Maybe when you come to my home or whatever we can read the Bible together and discuss it, or do you have a better suggestion?

Me: OK, first thing about touching. I felt comfortable at first, but if we do it pretty long like we did, I become uncomfortable. Anyway, I think it is good idea if I go to your home and we could discuss, but remember I know almost nothing about God. But I'm sure you understand, don't you darling?

David: Yes, I understand, but what shall we discuss?

Me: Honestly, I dunno what.

David: I could find a verse then we could discuss,

OK? I'll find a better way as we go. I want to ask you a question.

Me: Fine, but don't be embarrassed if I got the answer off the point.

David: No, it isn't about God. It is between you and me.

Me: Fine. What is it, sweetie?

David: If I touch your body for a short time, when it is right time (nobody is watching) do you mind? Or do you prefer I do nothing until you let me? Those questions are stupid; never mind answering. Let's talk about something else, like getting married. Ha ha! Just kidding.

Me: Very funny, but I won't ignore the question. I really dunno, but I prefer you ask me if it's alright to touch my body, then maybe I'll say OK. For your information, it'll be a long time before I let you do this, but I'm sure I'll let you once before I turn sixteen. I dunno, OK? OK, I don't care if you touch my ***, but I prefer not inside my clothing. OK, honey?

David: Thanks for answering my stupid question. What are you going to do after I finish talking with my dearie?

Me: I'll talk with Tiffany, then I suppose I'll read the book a little. What time are you planning to stop?

David: By nine, so I can do my homework. Are you finished talking with me? I think I talked long enough. Did you get bored?

Me: No way. For your information, I never become

bored with you. Ha! But it's true. Of course it's alright to stop darling. Homework is more important than me. Ha. So I think you better do your homework now. Sleep well tonight and think about me before you doze off. Ha! Bye. See you tomorrow. I love you and always will.

David: First of all, you are more important than homework, and second, how do you like the idea of talking about God?

Me: I think it's a great idea if you like it, but don't teach me about God when you don't want to. Of course, you'll not teach me all night when I'm at your home. Ha!

David: OK, sleep tight and may God be with you all night. See you in the morning. I love you. I don't have to tell you; you already know. Ha! Bye. GA or SK [TTY code for Stop Key]

Me: Wait, wait! You don't have to tell me, but I like it when you tell me. Tell me the truth, do you want to discuss with me a little about God? If not, just tell me. I'll understand. I can learn about Him later in my life. GA

David: It is better to learn about Him now. I'm crying. I'm worried about you. I want you to go to heaven with me. I can't see what I'm saying, so I'll see you tomorrow. I love you. Better stop now. Bye to SK

Me: Thanks for your concern. You are so sweet. Bye. SK

David: Are you still there? Is that all you can say? I'm crying. I want you to go to heaven with me. GA

Me: Don't worry. I'll go there with you. Do your homework now. See you tomorrow. I love you! SK

David: You don't want to know about God. Bye. SK

Me: No, wait. You still there? GA

David: Yes. GA

Me: I want to know more. I cry often at home when my mom won't take me to church. I tried my best, last summer, reading the Bible, but I still don't understand. OK? I just remembered one verse saying those who love xxx whoever … I forgot the verse now, but it is John 3 something like this. GA

David: OK. I'll talk more tomorrow. Bye. SK

Me: I do want to go to heaven. SK

David: I want you to accept Christ. Bye. SK

Me: I'm already a Christian. SK

Chapter 13

October 1983

Thump. Thump. We could feel the vibration of the big bass drum as we entered through the doors. Within minutes, our gym was filled with high school students, coaches, dormitory staff, teachers, and a few alumni. *Thump. Thump.* The cheerleaders did their pom-pom dance as we cheered. The bonfire would follow shortly, but first, we waited eagerly for the homecoming court to be announced.

Our superintendent opened the envelope and announced: "Freshman princess goes to Deanne Piper!" We all cheered as Deanne climbed down the steps to the middle of the gym, where five chairs were set. She sat down in the chair furthest left, facing the spectators.

"Sophomore princess goes to Amy Monigan!" Another round of applause. She sat down next to Deanne.

"Junior princess goes to Debbie Anderson!"

Slaps on my back and words of congratulations surrounded me as I got up from my seat, maneuvered through the crowd in the stands, and walked across the gym floor to take my seat. Emotions flooded in – thrilled to be chosen, relieved that I was not overlooked, and self-conscious that all eyes were now on me. I had hoped I'd be chosen although I hated standing before a crowd.

After naming Lori Sherwood as a Senior Princess, the superintendent announced: "Queen goes to Debbie Stokes!" Debbie hugged each of us before she took her seat.

At the bonfire, David and I held hands. The night had been

so pretty – stars filled the sky, and the night air was crisp. The bonfire burned high into the air as a large crowd of us stood hand-in-hand around the fire, moving slowly and occasionally stopping to sing familiar cheerleader chants.

When it was past ten o'clock, our dormitory counselor encouraged us to begin moving; it was time to return to our dorm. David and I walked across the campus, still holding hands.

As we neared my dorm, David turned to me and said: "I want to talk to you about something."

"Sure. What is it?" I asked.

"I want for us to be just friends."

"Friends? You mean, you want to break up with me?" We had dated for over two years and had so much fun together. We played miniature golf. I had gone to his house several times for supper. His parents liked me. We often went out for drives through town. (He had a car of his own, earning money from his paper route.) He even had a picture of me printed on a shirt that he wore all the time. Not only that, he often gave me small gifts, stuffed animals and Smurfs. I thought he would be mine forever. I even fantasized what our wedding would look like. And now, he was breaking up with me. I never dreamed this would happen.

"Right. I think it's best that we are just friends – for now."

"Why?" I looked at him, not comprehending. "There's nothing wrong with us. Did I do something wrong? You always said you loved me." It wasn't as if we had fought or anything. What was happening?

"I thought I did, but now I don't have feelings for you. Actually, your name is in the bottom part of my heart," he said bluntly.

I burst into tears.

He stood awkwardly and said, "I think I better go now."

After he walked away, I sat down on the steps to the administration building next to the lot where his car was parked, and stayed for I don't know how long. Why had he chosen this night to break up? Couldn't he have waited until after the homecoming weekend?

"Are you okay?" my dorm counselor asked when she found me there, hugging my knees, tears streaming down my cheeks. She sat next to me and asked: "Did someone say something cruel to you about your being a princess?"

"No, it's not that."

After several minutes of silence, she asked, "Do you want to talk?"

"No." We remained silent for several more minutes before she said we needed to return to the dorm.

The following day – our homecoming – David and I acted as if nothing had happened. No one knew. I went through the day with a fake smile.

"Hey, I want to take a picture of you two," people kept saying, so we posed. We looked good together – a football player and a junior homecoming princess.

By the following Monday morning, everyone knew our relationship had ended.

Chapter 14

Fall 1983 to Spring 1984

*I*t had never occurred to me that there might be a time when David and I would not be together. Immediately after our break-up, it wasn't so bad. We continued to do the things we had normally done: eating, talking, and laughing together. But then, he would ignore me for weeks at a time. Eventually he would come back, telling me how much he missed me. "Just a hug, please," he would beg, and that often led to a kiss. Some days, he would say that he still loved me. Other times, though, he would say that he didn't even know what love was.

After four months of this back-and-forth, he got a new girl-friend. To my horror, Elena snatched his jacket from my room without asking. It was a piece of clothing that had become my property, and I wanted to keep it. But the betrayals continued. My circle of close friends began to report their doings and whereabouts, assuring me that they were on my side. They were trying to be helpful, but none of us realized that I was better off not knowing all the details.

I was an emotional wreck. I never knew I was capable of crying so much. Everywhere I went, I cried – and couldn't stop. I cried in my dorm room, in the bathroom stall, in between classes, in the gym during practice, and in the classroom. Teachers, staff, and coaches were concerned about me, but no one really pushed me to talk; not that I would have opened up easily. Instead, they would tell me to try and forget him, or to focus on more important things, such as schoolwork. Perhaps everyone left it for my parents to handle. Or perhaps they assumed I would confide in my parents. Sadly, Mom's typical response to my tears was: "You still cry over David? Get over it. There are plenty of boys out there." I couldn't talk to Dad either. Though he was more on the soft side, he wouldn't know what to say. Neither one of them was capable of helping me cope with my overwhelming feelings. The only one who really listened was my overweight, smooth-haired dachshund, Cocoa. I would hold him against my chest, and he would lick my tears. It was as if he understood my pain.

While I was at school, I journaled about my heartache. I would write down my feelings in a blue spiral notebook – the same one I used for taking notes in one of my classes. I'd decided the best way to move forward was to just ignore David, so I quit talking to him altogether. I was worried about the busy spring, and how I would handle getting through all those important events without him, especially prom. I just couldn't believe I wouldn't be going with David. Since my freshman year, my friends and I had watched the upperclassmen gather in front of the water fountain for pictures – a prom tradition. Excitement was evident, and I had looked forward to my turn, with David.

On May 15, I wrote in my diary:

Prom is coming in two days. I don't know how I'll react. Maybe I'll cry. Maybe I'll not. I forgot what it's like to hold his hand. It's hard. I still love him, and I guess I still want him back.

Two days later, I wrote:

I've been worried sick about today since February. I thought I would cry and cry. But I didn't. It's amazing. I guess I got used to seeing them together. David looked good. Seven months of crying was enough. I look forward to summer, that's when I'll not cry for three whole months. Good way to get back to my old self.

To my surprise and delight, David broke up with Elena a few days after the prom. After forty-three days of silence, he begged me to talk to him. I gave in. On May 23, I journaled:

> So great talking to him! Walked with him from gym
> to cafeteria. We talked, but I left, because I didn't
> want him to think he has me to himself too much. We
> laughed ... I wish I could have him back. Everyone
> asked if we got back together. I wish. Thank you, God.

I thought I was getting stronger, but I was mistaken. I had foolishly let him hug and kiss me, only to learn that he didn't want me back. My crying spells returned, and I cried for four straight days. Again, I vowed that I would never speak to him! I was back to square one.

This time a teacher showed real concern. He asked if I wanted to talk. "No, I'm fine," I responded, though I frequently thought about his offer during the first two weeks of my summer vacation. *Perhaps, he is the one I could talk to.*

After writing several drafts, perfecting each version, I finally folded the letter, sealed it in an envelope, addressed it to him, placed it in our black mailbox, and raised the red flag.

Chapter 15

April 1989

I quickly realized it was a waste of time to look for the perfect dress. The most beautiful ones were very expensive. And I couldn't justify that, especially knowing it would only be worn less than eight hours.

As Mom and I stood in the room filled with racks containing hundreds of white and ivory dresses, I instructed her, "Look at each price tag *before* pulling it off the rack."

We had traveled to a bridal store in Chambersburg, Pennsylvania, hoping that the prices would be cheaper than in Hagerstown, our hometown. Instead of looking for the perfect dress, I hunted for the best price possible. Not what most brides would normally do, but for me, it was the way we did things.

The sales lady made such a fuss when I stepped out of the dressing room in one of the dresses. *Would she tell me honestly if the dress didn't look good on me?* I wondered. She led me to an area surrounded by tall panels of mirrors. I looked at myself in the reflection and I had to admit: I looked pretty, although I would have preferred a different style and design.

"It's perfect," Mom said.

Mom did not have a wedding dress when she married Dad. I had seen the picture. Mom wore a navy blue skirt with a matching jacket, and Dad wore his black suit. When I was a little girl, I was puzzled as to why she didn't have a traditional white dress. After I peppered her with questions, Mom finally showed me a thick laminated newspaper clipping that she had hidden under the lining in her drawer. The newspaper contained a picture of

Mom in a beautiful wedding dress announcing her marriage –
to a different man. Why she kept the clipping was beyond me.

My questions didn't stop there. Mom shared with me horror stories of what her first husband did to her, which led to a
divorce ten months later. She insisted that I keep this a secret
from my siblings, which I have never violated. Mom eventually
told my siblings about her divorce when they were older, but I
don't think she shared the sordid details.

Secrets. They're nothing new. Everyone has secrets, I suppose. I have mine.

Chapter 16

Summer 1984

July 10

Dear Debbie,

It was great getting a letter from you. You really do write a nice letter. It appears that you would rather write to me instead of talk. I guess that is okay, just as long as we communicate, that is the *important* thing.

I don't think what David thinks is important. What you think and feel is important. You have to decide if you want him back or not. It has to be your decision. Only you can decide that.

I think if you let yourself, you'll get over David, but you have to let yourself. I think you are a great person for still liking him after the ways he has hurt you this past year. Most girls would end up hating him.

I told you before, I am always willing to listen to you. I like you more than you realize and our conversations are completely secret and safe with me. Just don't build a stone wall between us.

Have a nice vacation. Thanks for writing – keep it up.

* * *

July 16

Debbie,

It was really nice hearing from you, and I did not need a cup of coffee to help me keep awake. Like I told you, you write a beautiful letter. I really enjoyed reading it. You have excellent language skills.

You can still relax and have your mind on David. That is not a real problem. However, you do have to keep your mind open and let yourself think of other things. I know it is not easy, but I'm sure you can do it.

Maybe David did love you once. In fact, I'm sure he did. But times change and people do too. It appears that David changed for some reason and stopped "loving" you. From what you said in your letter, your relationship with him was very normal. Most teenage relationships go through the same stages that you and David did.

From what you've said, it seems as if David is taking advantage of you. You had told me that you and he did not go all the way, but the day you went to David's house is unclear. Did you finally "go all the way" or just touch? It appears David knows when he has a good thing. He knows that you still like him and will accept him back anytime. So when he is [lusting] and wants some loving, he comes back to you. I think you have to set the rules.

I know you want him back, but for your sanity and reputation, you can't let him come back only when he wants to "touch" you. If he wants to kiss you then he has to come back as your boyfriend, not as a person you know.

You *are not* a cheap girl, but if you continue to let David do what he wants, you will become cheap. David knows that you are very pretty and have a nice body and he does not want to lose a good thing, so he keeps you hanging on so that he can have you when he wants you.

That is why I said for you to set the rules. You'll have to control the relationship. Also, I wouldn't chase him or call him. If he wants to come back, he should play by your rules. David is right about one thing, friends don't do things like that.

The reasons for breaking up – well, what you have listed are good reasons. The reason that sooner or later you'd have sex and both of you didn't want that is really not a good one, because like I said, you and David were going through stages in your relationship just like other couples do. You both would become more flexible and you both would want it. You may feel guilty afterward, but you would still want it. That is very normal.

I think that the reason he called you was because he felt guilty – a little bit. I don't think it was because he still loved you. There are different kinds of taking advantage, and in this situation he is taking advantage of you and your feelings.

I think that David's attitude would change a lot if he knew that he could not get you whenever he wanted to get you.

I hope I've made some sense to you. You know I prefer to talk. And I am glad that you didn't throw the letter away like the others. See, you should have written me a long time ago.

Hope to hear from you soon. Say hi to your parents for me.

Someday I'll ask you to define touching, etc.

* * *

July 31

Dear Debbie,

Well, I'm back from our vacation.

I know that being needed by friends is not the same as a boyfriend or girlfriend. People always need to be loved. There are very few people in the world who do not need to be loved.

I never knew about your parents, that is a surprise. I never would have guessed that. Well, you can always start by hugging them. Maybe they don't know how; you can teach them. You start hugging them and see what happens. I know you don't like to let me hug you. Each time I try you always push me away. Maybe because it is like you said, I'm "a male teacher." Or is it because I am old and fat?

I know that it does feel good to get some love and attention. We all need it … including male teachers – fat and old. Ha, ha!!!

I think one problem you have is that you have too many people keeping you informed about David and what he does, who he talks to, and so on; if you know what I mean. People should leave you alone. I think that will help.

I'll never ask you to define touching – enough said!!!

Take care, write soon!!!

* * *

August 13

Dear Debbie,

It was nice having two letters waiting for me when I got back. Sorry I didn't answer your letter, but I had to make a quick trip to see my brother and was not able to let you know. Of course I like writing to you. Don't be silly.

About the hugging, well, of course you let me hug you on the last day of school; everyone was hugging you, you didn't have a choice. I always have a reason for hugging you – I CARE!!! And I want to let you know that you always have a friend in me, and if you can't or won't hug your parents, you can always hug me. You can try to help your parents. Maybe they need to be shown how to hug their children – try it. It's never too late.

Good luck with your job, if you got it. What is it and what will you be doing? You didn't say in your letter.

I hope that you try thinking positive regarding yourself and your relationship with David. I think it is very important for your sake. Like I said in one of my other letters, you have to set the rules and control the situation. You cannot let the situation control you. David will take advantage of you if you let him. He can't take advantage of you if you don't let him. You have to understand that and follow through with it.

Couple of questions: Would it really be the end of the world if David never came back to you? What would you do and how would you feel if you and David never got back together?

You don't have to answer if you don't want to. I'm just surprised that you are still that upset about David. The pain should be less by now.

Take care. Say hi to your parents and granny too.

Hug them!!!

* * *

I responded to his letter with a poem.

> *Avoiding his hugs*
>   *When he asks, "What is wrong?"*
> *I tell him, "Not important enough for you to know."*
>   *He was hurt.*
> *It hurts me to know I hurt him.*
>   *When I needed to talk, I wrote him notes because*
> *I just couldn't talk to him.*
>   *Since I prefer to write instead of talk, he said,*
> *"As long as we communicate, that is the most impor-*
> *tant thing."*
>   *Then, I wrote him a nine-page letter*
> *Telling him almost everything.*
>   *It may be the dumbest thing I ever did*
> *But he said that I wrote a beautiful letter*
>   *And that I had excellent language.*

What a relief!
   Since he said I could trust him,
I started to express my feelings
   And he shared his opinions.
After getting his first letter,
   I looked forward to the next one.
His last letter arrived two Wednesdays ago–
   He talked about the subject of hugging.
I wrote him back telling him
   I don't mind him hugging me.
Yes, it's true.
   I've always enjoyed his affection
But I never wanted him to know.
   Don't ask why – I don't understand it myself.
I also told him,
   "Please remember: if you are doing it for my sake,
Please don't write."
   Maybe I wanted to hear him saying,
"No, I love and enjoy writing to you."
   I sent him the letter and didn't hear back.
I wrote him another one.
   Telling him I wanted to see or call my loved one.
And that it wasn't fair for my loved one not to be my
good friend.
   Oh, I was upset by then.
Now, I haven't heard back from him and
   I wonder why he didn't write.
Getting his letters meant a lot to me.
   I guess I grew to love him
Not in a romantic way
   But I love him as if he is my dad!
Since I didn't get his letter,
   I might not write another one.

Then, I started to daydream a lot about my loved one.
  I started to cry once in a while because
I wanted to see or call my loved one.
  Oh, why didn't he write?
I'll push him away
  When he tries to hug me.
I'll say, "Not important enough for you to know,"
  When he asks what's wrong.
Writing him letters,
  I felt so much better.
Not until I haven't heard back,
  I started crying again.
Oh, help me–
  Write me one more time so
I'll have someone to trust during my last year at school.

* * *

August 16

Dear Debbie,

It is always great hearing from you. Because I am late or slow in answering your letters does not mean that I don't think about you, because I do.

Some jobs are boring, but the money is good. Just keep smiling and do a good job.

Don't worry about not being disciplined. Your parents have done a wonderful job in raising you. I don't know about your sister and brother, but I do know you. They have done a good job; you are a fine young lady. I am sure that they love you and are very proud of you. You are lucky to have nice parents. Just help your parents as much as you can. And don't be embarrassed about them. Remember you are getting a better education than they did. Also help your brother and sister. You don't have to take all the responsibility, but just be supportive and help your parents when they don't understand something.

It's alright to daydream – keep on; just don't live in a dream world all the time. Walt Disney once said, "A dream is a wish your heart makes." I've always liked that quote. Just don't live in a dream world.

Don't worry about crying; you'll be okay in time. You'll stop crying. Things will get better.

Your poem is great. I really loved it. I also like hearing from you. I really do care about you. I feel closer to you than I do to others. I don't know why, maybe because you have the prettiest legs, ha ha. But I do feel close to you. I feel embarrassed if I took your father's place, but I'm glad that you feel close to me. I love you too, and not in a romantic way. You are too old for me, ha ha! Save your poem; it is filled with a lot of honest emotions – a wonderful job. I really hate to see you graduate. Wish you could stay a few more years.

Our summer friendship will last a long time, don't worry. I'll always be around for you, and I'll still want to hug you, even for no reason; just to let you know I'm still here.

Chapter 17

Fall 1984

*T*rue to his word, he continued to be there for me through the autumn. And I found myself depending on this new relationship more and more:

> *You provided me a special friend*
>> *Who is always there to listen*
> *Yes, it helped me a lot*
>> *Without this friend,*
> *I probably would keep things inside.*
>> *When school started,*
> *We didn't talk that much*
>> *But I wrote him notes anyhow.*
> *It seems as if our special friendship is fading.*
>> *Why am I sometimes mad*
> *When there's a girl*
>> *Who seems like she wants to have*
> *This special friend I've gotten.*
>> *Is it right for me to feel mad and jealous?*
> *It's just that*
>> *This person is a special friend God provided.*
> *He showed he cared about me.*
>> *That's all I need to know…*
> *Someone cares.*

* * *

It's nice to have a friend
*   You think is special*
Who thinks of you
*   The same.*

What a warm feeling
*   That spreads all around you*
When he said nice things
*   That meant just for you.*

Smile spreads on your face
*   Just because you're happy*
To have him as a friend
*   Who is there to understand you.*

Sighing out a relief
*   When your feelings and thoughts*
Were set free
*   Knowing he'll keep them to himself.*

So comforting
*   When he hugs you and says he loves you.*
But not in a romantic way, he says
*   That makes you laugh.*

Great feeling
*   Knowing he likes you*
The way you are
*   And cares for you.*

Thinking of the wonderful friendship
*   You two have been developing*
That will always
*   Remain dearly in your heart!*

Chapter 18

Christmas Day 1984

*D*arryl, who had graduated from MSD three years earlier, invited me to a New Year's Eve party in New York. I knew he liked me, but I was never interested in him. I was uncomfortable with the idea of going, but Mom wasn't. When I told her about it, she said I could go. Bridgetta begged me to accept his invitation, given that she had a boyfriend in New York and wanted to tag along. But after her parents checked around, they said no. Relieved, I used her as the excuse I needed to decline Darryl's invitation.

However, David had heard that I was considering, and he was not happy:

David: Hi. David here. GA

Me: Hi there again. I just couldn't go and let the call ruin me on Christmas day, so I'm calling you again. I'm curious what business it was for you to be mad when you found out I was invited to be with Darryl for New Year's? GA

David: It wasn't my business. You are right. There is nothing wrong with that.

Me: Yeah, but can you tell me why you got uptight over this?

David: I'm just shocked that he invited you and you accepted. That's all.

Me: Oh come on. Tell me what's bothering you?

David: I said nothing. I was just shocked. If you told someone else they would be shocked too; that's normal.

Me: Yeah, but you said last night that you were mad. Why?

David: That was last night when I found out, then I realized nothing was wrong with that.

Me: What did the statement mean: my heart is beating so hard?

David: Of course, when you are shocked or can't believe something, your heart beats, plus I was extra surprised that it was you, so it beat so fast.

Me: **** it. Do you believe that I want to be with that boy??? Bridgetta wanted to see Greg and pleaded with me to make her dream come true. To make her happy and since I had nothing to do, I called Darryl and told him Bridgetta and I would go. I was scared at first, but apparently Bridgetta answered my prayers when she called and said she couldn't go.

David: OK, then why did you want … forget it. OK, I see the whole point now. That is better, OK?

Me: I cried recently and you shouldn't be surprised. Oh well. I really do want to see you. **** you. Why are you always there when I'm … whatever.

David: I'm sorry if I'm in your way. I'll wait until college to say goodbye to each other.

Me: Oh, don't say that. I don't ever want to think of that really. Did you mean it when you said why not go steady again? Don't worry. I'll say no anyhow, but I'm just curious.

David: Forget what I said. The whole thing was stupid. That's part of the reason why I am avoiding seeing you tomorrow, because you will want to hold me and etc.

Me: Oh yeah, you're blaming me for all of this. Thanks a lot. Why do you have to hurt me so much?

David: I was not blaming anyone and didn't mean to hurt you. I'm really sorry about everything.

Me: Oh man, you said that thousands of times. What has gotten into you? A Christian boy? I guess I'm a better person, yet I don't go to church. What do they teach in churches??? Oh I'm sorry; I didn't mean that.

David: Yes, of course you're a better person than me. I'm still a kid who likes to be a little devilish sometimes. I can't wait until I grow up.

Me: I wish I could just die. Why can't we be friends? Why can't we be? I wish we didn't do things last Thursday. **** it. Why did I let this happen?

David: I just wanted to hug you for some affection, but we somehow got deeper. It was not my goal to go deeper; it seems as if Satan tempted us.

Me: We can't let that continue unless you love me, which you never did. I just want to make sure for one more time. Maybe I thought it was just a dream. Are we going to prom definitely or maybe or what?

David: Yes, if we can be happy and have fun for once.

Me: You say if? How do you know that we will not have fun?

David: OK, I think if we continue like friends, we have fun. Then why not have fun at prom, too? I'm sure there will be no problems, so you better get busy and start looking for your prom dress.

Me: Two people will die if you cancel the whole thing. I'll kill you first before killing myself.

David: That won't happen, OK?

Me: Oh sure. Why didn't you respect me enough to leave me alone until the pain was gone? Every time I get better you hurt me again. Every time you hurt me, the more I hate you. Part of why I wanted to see you tomorrow is that I want us to do something that will hurt me again. That way I'll hate you completely.

David: We won't see each other tomorrow.

Me: Yeah I know, but it hurts for some reason. Really, I really wanted to see you. I don't only love you as a boyfriend, but you were my best friend too. I enjoyed talking to you. Can't you understand that?

David: Yes, I have lots fun with you, but why not take the word *love* out of your heart just like me? I don't know what love is.

Me: That's the problem. You don't know, so how can you command me to take my love out? Can you tell your mom to take her love out for your dad?

David: Oh no, they know what it means and they are using it the right way. It seems that you are abusing yourself. I think that's silly. I think you should enjoy life like what I'm doing, but I'm not going too far.

Me: It seems like you never try to understand me. Just

give a try and accept me the way I am. Why can't you? You make me so confused. You wrote what a beautiful lady I was in my senior picture. Tell me to forget that and you didn't mean that.

David: That's true, you are beautiful. Same as Bridgetta looks beautiful. Tiffany looks beautiful. I am handsome, same as Joey, Roger, and Charles. So … if I am not able to understand you, then go to someone who does.

Me: But you don't tell that to Tiffany or Bridgetta, do you?

David: Yes, I tell them they are beautiful.

Me: Oh yeah, they didn't tell me. Are you making that up? I dunno. Whatever it is, it doesn't matter. The point is that the pain is the same, and I tried, I really tried, to get over you. I could have succeeded if you didn't bother me. Maybe you didn't realize, but I took it seriously when you said nice things to me. Please try not to bother me; it hurts. It really does. Try to leave me alone, OK?

David: Yes. Are you still there? What did you say in the end?

Me: Try to leave me alone.

David: OK. I'll try. Just like the last four weeks?

Me: It's hard for me to say yes because I hate those four weeks. All I want is for you to try to understand me. Try to be reasonable. Yes, I want us to be friends. But don't say such nice things. Just nothing, please. Don't ever tempt me by giving me hugs or asking me out unless you promise yourself not to do anything. Clear?

David: I'll try my best. OK, fine. Then see you at the prom.

Me: Are we still going together?

David: Silly question.

Me: Ha, ha. Oh, OK.

David: Since you don't want to talk seriously, I will just say simple things to you as if I was talking to Tiffany or Bridgetta. Is that what you want?

Me: I dunno. I just want us to be true and good friends. I want us to talk like we used to, but I don't want to do things like hugging.

David: Fine, that is clear. OK.

Me: OK, fine. I guess that's all I called for. GA or SK

David: OK, see you. Bye. SK

Chapter 19

February 1985

I crumpled the sheet of paper and threw it in the wastebasket. It was my fourth or fifth attempt at writing. I reached for another sheet and paused, trying to think of a different approach to begin my letter.

A few days earlier, David and I had gone out for a drive around the town. When he brought me back to the campus, he was frustrated because I had resisted his kiss. I no longer allowed him to do whatever he pleased. It had been a year and three months since our break up, and I had finally gotten stronger.

"So, you have a new boyfriend?" David asked.

"Oh, right," I said sarcastically. "I have a boyfriend. You are jealous, huh?"

"So what if I'm jealous?"

"You're so dumb. Who would I go out with?" I challenged him. He knew I wasn't interested in anyone, except him.

"I bet you thought of what it would be like to kiss *him,*" he said, shocking me.

"That's disgusting." I looked at him in disbelief; how could he think of such a thing?

"I bet it's true. If not, why wouldn't you let me kiss you?"

"You're so s-i-c-k! You know, you've changed so much. It's as if I don't know you anymore," I said and opened the passenger door to get out.

"Oh, come on. You know I really didn't mean that. Come back," he coaxed me.

"Forget it. I'm leaving." I shut the door and walked away. My feelings for David had changed slowly over time. I was actually scared of what I was feeling. I had written a poem earlier:

> Slowly, my feelings had changed.
>> From days into weeks into months.
> I had wanted this to happen
>> And it did!
> But it scares me.
>> Is my mind working right?
> I used to pretend that I don't love him anymore.
>> Right now, I think it's true.
> Yes, I love him.
>> But I don't feel the way I used to.
> Does that mean I don't love him anymore?
>> Scary thought.
> I never thought it would happen.
>> What if I really still love him?
> He's getting crazy over me again,
>> And I'm not so thrilled about this.
> Yes, it's terrific,
>> But I am taking things easy.
> Is it because
>> I know he would leave me again?
> Or is it because my feelings are no longer there?

I tried to concentrate as I began writing on a new sheet of paper. My thoughts drifted to my conversation with David. What he said the other night caught me off guard. At that moment I sincerely thought what he said was gross, but as the days passed, I took a hard look at myself and had to admit that what he said was true. I had thought about what it would be like to kiss... *him.*

I felt guilty. How could I have such thoughts? He was a

teacher. Not to mention that he was also married. I knew what I had to do – tell him the truth. I was not sure I could go on pretending my thoughts did not exist and suffering with the guilt. How would he react? I just hoped that he would forgive me, and that it wouldn't jeopardize our friendship. A risky confession.

At last, I was satisfied with the letter I wrote. I folded it several times before placing it securely inside the pocket of my jeans. Now, I had to figure out the right time to pass on the note.

Chapter 20

August 1989

I stood in front of the full-length mirror, and the soon-to-be bride stared back at me. In a few minutes, a new chapter in my life would begin. Only two years ago I thought I would be doomed to a life of being single. *If only I had waited...*

My thoughts were interrupted when someone gently touched my shoulder. I saw Dad's reflection, letting me know that it was time to go. I quickly glanced once more at the soon-to-be-bride, making sure nothing was out of place before departing.

We walked toward the anteroom that would lead us into the sanctuary – an early twentieth century great hall with wooden pews and beautiful stained glasses on both sides. The church had played a significant role in our family throughout the years. Grandma, my uncles, and my siblings grew up in this congregation. And while Mom, Dad, and I could not participate, Dad had helped build the pipe organ whose melody now would guide us down the aisle.

I looked at Dad and reminded him: "I need to be on your left side, remember."

"Yes, that's right." Dad walked around my train, and when he reached my right side, he stopped abruptly. I saw an expression on his face I didn't recognize; he clearly wanted to say something but didn't quite know how. He was not a man of many words.

"Would it be OK if I kiss you on the cheek when I give you away?" Dad blurted out.

His request caught me off guard. He had never kissed me before. Not wanting to hurt his feelings, I replied: "That'll be fine."

Why Dad chose this moment to give me a kiss, I'll never know. I wished he didn't. His kiss felt awkward and artificial. Did he feel pressured, knowing it was customary to kiss the bride when giving her away?

Chapter 21

February 1985

I leaned my left cheek against the cold window of our school van as six of us traveled to Madison Square Garden for the U.S.A. Mobil Indoor Track and Field Championship meet in New York. Our coach, Jack Griffin, had gotten us tickets and declared that this event would be one we'd never forget.

We left early Friday morning; our principal granted us special permission to miss school. As Mr. Griffin drove, our excitement was evident. The girls talked about the different athletes we would witness competing – one of them being Carl Lewis. I was rather quiet on the ride; however, my mind was replaying what had taken place the night before.

I had stood by the door and smiled nervously when he saw me.

"Come in. What's up?" He said, looking at the clock. "Aren't you going to see the game?"

"I still have time. It's not 6:30 yet." I was on my way from the dorm to the gym to watch the varsity boys' basketball game when I noticed that the light in his classroom was on. I wanted to give him the note now, or else I'd have to wait until the following week because of our trip to New York. I didn't want to wait.

"Is everything okay? Did you want to talk?" he asked.

"No." I took the note out of my jeans' pocket and said: "I have a note for you."

"I know you prefer to write. But you're here now. Couldn't you just tell me?"

I shook my head. "I prefer you read." After I handed him the note, I was about to walk out of the classroom.

"Wait," he stopped me. "Why don't you just stay while I read? Then, maybe we can talk about it?"

"Okay," I sighed. It was not going to be easy, but he was right. Perhaps, it was best we talked about it in person to just get it over with.

As he unfolded the note, I looked down at the floor, ashamed of what he was going to find out. After he finished reading, he lifted my face to meet his eyes, and assured me: "Please don't feel guilty. It's okay. There's nothing to forgive."

"But it's wrong," I said.

"I'm not sure about that," he said. "You are not the only one, you know."

I looked at him, not comprehending.

"I've wanted to kiss you since last November," he confessed.

"Since November?"

He nodded.

And, so we did.

Chapter 22

February 1985

After our kiss, everything changed.
Everything.

Not gradually, but overnight.

I had never felt constant fear before then. I was worried that our affection was too obvious. I worried that my classmates would suspect that something was going on between the two of us. In the past, I would pass notes to him via my classmates, even teacher-aides, without much thought. Now I would only hand-deliver them. I became paranoid as well. Every time someone mentioned his name, I was extra careful with my responses.

I learned how to lie. The minute I got home from school on Fridays, I would have to come up with reasons why I needed the car. Fridays at 4:00 p.m. was the only time we could sneak out to be together. Every time I lied about my whereabouts, the easier it rolled off my hands. At times, I surprised myself with how creative my lies were, or how quickly I came up with them.

I put up a facade. I continued to push him away when he tried to hug me. I brushed him off when he complimented me. I laughed along with my classmates when they teased him – the way we tease teachers. I ignored him, perhaps to an extreme, just to alleviate suspicion.

After our kiss, things progressed quickly. The first time he caressed me – in places I'd never been touched – I was scared, but I managed not to show it. I experienced physical feelings I never knew existed. He was much older, over twice my age, and I trusted him.

He was the first adult to say three simple yet powerful words to me – words that my parents had never said: "I love you."

He made me feel special.

I was loved.

I was desired.

I was beautiful.

I was intelligent.

And he even gave me a special nickname – *Lady.*

He had become the father figure I had desperately needed. But now we were involved in ways I never knew would hurt me – almost kill me. It would be many years until I fully understood the depth of the deception.

Chapter 23

March 1985

I opened the envelope, holding my breath as I pulled out the letter.

Ms. Debbie L. Anderson
Route #3, Box 216
Williamsport, MD 21795

Dear Debbie:

Congratulations!

I made it into Gallaudet. What a relief!

I am very pleased to welcome you to the fall 1985 incoming freshman class.

Freshman. I was afraid I would have to begin in Gallaudet's pre-college preparatory program. But I made it to the Freshman class.

I am confident that among our more than thirty-three major programs (including majors such as Computer Science, Business Administration, Education, and Physical Education) you will find an excellent opportunity to meet your educational and career goals.

Your coming years will be exciting, rewarding, and meaningful as you prepare for your life and a satisfying career. At Gallaudet you'll have many opportunities.

Going to college was not part of my plan. If not for the insistence of several of my teachers and coaches, who had graduated from Gallaudet, I wouldn't have applied. The reasons were numerous.

I didn't think I was capable; in other words, I wasn't smart enough. Despite my being in the top class at MSD, I always felt my classmates were smarter than I was. My grades were not outstanding. I reasoned that it was safer not to apply – it would have been better to wonder whether I would have been accepted rather than to be rejected. I didn't think my pride could have handled it.

Where would I get the money? College cost money – a lot. Having grown up without much of it, I knew there was no question that Mom and Dad couldn't contribute a dime toward the tuition. I assumed that Grandma had money; Mom and Dad always asked her for it. But I resented them for borrowing and not paying back. I had decided a long time ago that I would not live like that.

Lastly, I have always carried the guilt of knowing I was smarter than my parents. I was concerned about how they would feel about my going to college. My feelings had run so deep that I would find myself subconsciously acting dumb around them just to reassure them that I was no better than they were. For instance: when they would ask what a word meant, I would simply tell them I wasn't sure. I would go to great lengths to get a dictionary and look up the definition of a word I already knew.

Despite my concerns, I filled out the application just to get the teachers and coaches off my back. Then, what a relief it was to receive the letter and to know I was accepted.

Chapter 24

May 1985

$\mathcal{I}$ suppose my life at home had always been *part* pretense. I had to be careful with my words. I had to hide my emotions. I had to act as if all was well. Now, my life was pretty much *all* pretense. And I was good at it. After all, years of practice makes one perfect.

On our dorm floor, I stood among my girlfriends as we dressed and helped each other get ready for our special evening – prom. It was an event I had looked forward to, yet now that the day had finally arrived, I was not there wholeheartedly. It was one more scene in which I had to play act.

When one of our dates would arrive at the door, someone would run up to get us. I stood waiting with the rest of my friends in my ankle-length, maroon dress, and as I waited, I touched the 14-karat gold necklace that hung around my neck. It was a surprise gift *he* had given me several weeks after our first kiss. I had asked what the gift was for. An all-sort-of-reasons celebration, he said. Nothing particular. He was just proud of me and my accomplishments: My upcoming graduation from MSD. My acceptance into Gallaudet. My being on the Deaf Olympic team, representing the USA at the upcoming World Games.

At last, my date had arrived. I walked down the stairs to our front lobby and stepped out the front door. David stood in his grey tuxedo with his bow and cummerbund matching the color of my dress. He was holding a pink corsage in his hand. When he saw me, he came forward and placed it over my wrist. In turn, I pinned a rose on his tuxedo. We then walked, arm in arm, toward the water fountain that stood in the middle of our campus, where everyone had gathered to take pictures. David's family was there with their camera to capture our special occasion. My family didn't come. They didn't ask if they could, and I didn't invite them.

He had wanted to come. Just for a few minutes, he asked, just to get a glimpse of me. But I told him not to. I did not want him there. He had said I was free to do whatever I pleased. "Just go and have fun," he had encouraged me. I had mixed feelings about the entire evening, but I knew one thing for sure: I didn't want him among the crowd of spectators. Perhaps I knew I would feel awkward with him watching. Perhaps I didn't want to deal with my guilt.

David and I posed in front of the fountain, my right arm through the loop of his left arm and our hands, my right and his right, intertwined. Next to David, was his sister who smiled at him affectionately. David's mother stood on my left, smiling broadly. David's father stood farthest to my left. One, two, three. Smile. Click. One, two, three. Smile. Click. There was always "Just one more picture."

The last time I had allowed David to kiss me had been back in December. Just a few days before our evening out, I had made it clear to him that my going with him to the prom did not mean he could have access to my lips. He understood, despite his declaration in February that he loved me and that he wouldn't give up on me.

Now that my love had been consumed by someone else, I felt stronger. Resisting David had suddenly become easy. I was now loved. Though I was still paranoid, and so secretive, I felt good, and happy.

Chapter 25

*D*ad and I made our grand entry into the sanctuary. When we stepped onto the aisle runner, we paused for several seconds.

Peter stood at the far end of the aisle, just below the chancel. I could see the joy radiating from his face as he waited eagerly to receive me as his bride. He was dressed handsomely in a black tuxedo. I smiled self-consciously as guests on both sides of the aisle stood and turned to face Dad and me.

Traditionally, the wedding ushers would sit the bride's family and guests on the left side of the church and the groom's family and guests on the right. But because only a few of Peter's family members and friends were able to travel to witness our wedding, our guests were not assigned to either side of the congregation. There was Uncle Dale, sitting just behind my cousin Tammy and her husband, Steve. My great aunt, Arvella, sat next to my cousin Sue Ellen and her husband, Glenn. Several of my high school classmates were present as well – Joey, David, Belinda, and Ed.

So many were there for our big day, including *him*. As much as I wanted to avoid seeing him, he was impossible to miss. There he stood, at the very end of the pew, right next to the aisle where I would pass shortly.

He was dressed in sky-blue pants and a short-sleeve white, buttoned shirt; his Sunday best.

He stood alongside his wife. Our eyes met, and after a second or two, I looked away.

Little did I know he would be the source of my trauma for years to come.

Chapter 26

I paced, keeping my eye on the phone light. If it was out of my sight, I wouldn't be able to see it ringing. I didn't want Mom to answer the phone.

I walked from our den to the dining room. I had wanted to go out today just to touch our initials. We had gone to Dam 4 the other day and walked along the C & O canal. With a knife he'd brought along, he carved a heart with our initials on a tree, for the world to see. I was his. He was mine. But I had taken the car yesterday and I didn't want to come up with another excuse as to why I needed it today.

Dining room into the kitchen. Yesterday I had called him at home, hoping we could talk. But someone answered and hung up; probably one of his kids. I didn't think he'd be at work since it was a Saturday, but thought I'd take the risk. I drove to MSD, but his vehicle was nowhere to be seen. Even though I had seen him only two days ago, it felt like a long time ago. *The hickey is still there.* After stopping by MSD, I wanted to go over to Power Line, our secret meeting place, but it was getting dark. Instead, I drove home, passing High's, where we ate ice cream the other day. His car wasn't there either. *Of course not, what did I expect?*

Kitchen into the living room. Tomorrow I would be leaving for Gallaudet. I wasn't sure if I would like it. All my classmates were looking forward to it. That was all they talked about before our graduation: Independence. Away from home. Drinking. New friends. Partying all night. Not me. I wasn't interested.

Actually, when my friends did things they weren't supposed to, such as drinking or smoking, I would report their doings to Mom and Dad. It was my way of seeking their approval. *Mom and Dad, look at me. I am a good girl. I don't smoke. I don't drink.* I wanted them to recognize what a good girl I was and praise me. But they didn't. *Gallaudet. I have no intention of getting involved in such activities. Will I find friends who are like me?*

Living room into the dining room. I wanted to see him! I had written him several letters. All of them were torn into pieces and thrown in the trash can. *What is he doing now? Snuggling with his wife while watching a TV show?* I couldn't help thinking more and more about him and her. How could I go on? *Is she good in bed? Does she taste better?* One day, I had become so bold as to ask him that question. His response: people tasted the same; it's the feelings that make the difference. *How could he kiss her?* Some days I couldn't bear the thought of him kissing her. Some days I was able to put my thoughts and feelings aside. Some days I just didn't care, as long as I had him.

Dining room into the den. Does he still love her? I had believed that he didn't. But now, I wasn't sure. Perhaps he still loved her. I know I loved him – no question. But, our love... how would I describe our relationship? Beautiful, yes. But, it was also frustrating and painful. If we continued to see each other, I knew our love would destroy me. Tomorrow, I'm leaving. What will happen to us? *Forgive me if I decide not to write. Forgive me if I decide to leave you.*

Den into the kitchen. He had said he was afraid he would lose me. Unbelievable. He was so much a part of me, and I wouldn't want to let him go. Beautiful. He made me feel so beautiful. He made everything seem beautiful. *Would it be possible for me to love someone else? If I ever do, I hope he will be like him.*

Kitchen into the dining room. Gallaudet. Will I like it there? At MSD, I saw him every day. At Gallaudet, I will not have a car. How often will we see each other? Nights and weekends are what I hate; those are the times we can't see each other. *I want to talk to him now. I need him. Right now. Not tomorrow or the day after.*

"What's the matter? You've been pacing around. Are you nervous? I thought you were excited?" Mom asked.

"Tiffany was supposed to call, but I guess she got tied up," I said.

The clock ticked, 9:58 p.m. He never called. Actually, he never said he would call, but I was hoping he would. *How could he not call on my last night home? My last night home! Why didn't he just find an excuse to call?*

Chapter 27

Fall 1985 – Freshman Year

*D*uring my first semester at Gallaudet, I kept a journal.

8-20-85

I find myself longing for him. How will I ever get rid of him? Not that I want to. But I just can't let it continue forever.

8-21-85

Not so exciting here. Met some new friends but, you know, just met them. David kept on hugging me and I just let him. I hope I am not giving him the wrong idea about us.

8-28-85

People dancing.
  Music vibrating.
Hands talking everywhere.
  In their hands they hold beer,
In the Abbey.

Watching them,
  No beer can in my hands,
Standing silently
  In the Abbey.

Drifting into thoughts of you.
  People cannot tell
For they can't see
  In the Abbey.

Thinking of you
  In the Abbey.

9-1-85

L oving you has been beautiful, but

O ften it's painful.

V ague feelings about

E verything.

9-9-85

Got his letter today. Brightens my day! I forget sometimes how great his love is. I need to stop thinking
about him and his wife; how unfair it is for him to
be with her. It's because I went out a few times with
Darryl. He introduced me to new experiences I've
never had, such as eating Chinese food. He will be out
of town for the weekend and said I could borrow his
car. I might go home to see *him!*

9-10-85, 1:52 a.m.

People here are enjoying themselves; at least they seem
to be having fun, laughing. I'm completely different
from them. Here I am at Gallaudet. New life. New
friends. New opportunity. New freedom. More education. But I'm not happy. I hate it here, but I don't get

to admit it. Seems like everyone loves to drink, smoke pot, get drunk, and laugh over dumb things. I just do not fit in. Not because I don't want to. I just simply can't. I don't feel comfortable around them.

Seeing my MSD friends drinking bothers me. Maybe I want them to be like me. I seem to be the only one here who is different. I don't smoke. I don't drink. I don't swear. Am I closed-minded? I wonder if the only way to make friends is to join in and drink? Should I? Drinking is dumb. I don't want to do that and I won't. But how can I go on here if I don't like it? I miss my MSD friends. I miss MSD – sports, friends, and teachers.

I want to just disappear to where no one knows me and start a new life. My life is already so messed up. But I can't just withdraw. People will look down at me. I might as well stay and suffer.

I miss him. Sometimes, I just wish I could go live with him. **** our situation.

9-11-85

I went crazy yesterday, crying all night from 11:30 p.m. to 2:00 a.m. Now I am feeling good. It's weird, really. Once in a while, I would cry and cry without stopping. My crying was because of many things. I really don't understand myself. I cried in David's room and kept on crying. We hugged, and late into the night, he asked me to stay overnight with him, but I came to my senses and left. Why did I let him hold me? I thought I was sure I didn't love him. Maybe it was just that I needed affection. I really don't know.

Going home today. Some days when I feel good, my being here is OK. Maybe it's because I know I will see him. Getting his letters and knowing I'm loved brightens my day. Other days, I just hate it here.

9-13-85

Felt so great! Happy! Because I saw him last night. I love him so much! I don't think I'll ever let him go. We almost did it last night, but for a change, it was he who said no.

9-15-85

I miss him. Thought of him a lot. Only six more days until I see him. I can't wait.

Three friends and I went to see a palm reader last night. My question: How will my love life turn out? Answer: I will get the one I truly love by the end of the year. He is the one I truly love. Does that mean he will leave his wife? Will he be mine forever?

I drank a pineapple daiquiri last night. Strawberry piña colada tonight. At the end, it tasted terrible. I won't drink ever again. Two experiences were enough.

9-16-85

Just got back from the cafeteria. I hate it here!!!! David passed by me in the cafeteria and said, "First time I see you here." That was all he said. Maybe I should transfer to NTID next year. New friends. New people. Nobody who knows me. Old classmates kept talking

about me and David. It's just that they know me. I
need to be in a different place where I can change. I
mean, start everything new.

9-24-85

I keep on asking myself what am I doing here? I feel
as if I'm wasting my time. I'm not as busy as everyone
would think a college student should be. At nights, I
tend to stay in my room doing absolutely nothing. I
have friends who exchange a few words as we pass by,
but when they have something to do, they don't think
of including me.

Saw a poster about Peace Corps. Must have been at
least eighteen years old. Maybe I could do that. The
thought of going to the Philippines is scary, but I want
to get out of here. The poster mentioned something
about having teaching experience. I'll have to check
this out.

I'm tired of my life. It has no meaning. No joy of living. Everything is just dull.

Later the same day, I got information about Peace
Corps. It said I must have college degree or have experience working in one of five fields. Oh, I wish I could
have this opportunity.

9-25-85

Can't wait until Friday to go home. Maybe I can find a
job somewhere. Will I be able to afford a place to live?

9-30-85

Just done lifting weights. I don't have much energy
left. I'm just tired of everything. Maybe it's my fault.
I don't socialize much. And I always go home on
weekends. After October 4th, I think I'll stay here until
November.

10-1-85

Two and a half more months until the semester is
over. I guess I'll stay through the year. Being on the
basketball team should help. (I hope I make it on the
team.)

Boring here. Life has no meaning. People say college
life is great. It's just a joke.

Got his letter today. I almost cried. It's because we
can't do many things together. And I always go home
on weekends to see him and we get together for such a
short time. I need to learn to stay here; maybe things
will get better. Not sure if I should end our relationship. It has to stop, but how? When? I don't want to,
but it may be best if I do. If it ever happens, I want us
to be very close friends. I don't want what happened
between David and me to happen again.

10-8-85

He'll call me in exactly an hour. I can't wait! The janitor asked yesterday if my boyfriend was going to call.
I told her yes, he'll call tomorrow (today). I guess the
last time he called, the joy radiated off my face.

I get headaches a lot lately. I don't get them at home.
But here, I get them often.

10-9-85

I'm feeling awful. Ate too much. I feel sick, both
physically and mentally. Maybe I'm lovesick too. He
never called yesterday. Must have been a good reason.
Maybe he had a last-minute meeting.

10-9-85

> *My heart is filled with pure love.*
> *A love for you,*
> *Just you!*
>
> *Although I know our love is so wrong,*
> *My heart seems like saying:*
> *If your love is strong,*
> *Let it flow freely.*
>
> *I kept on telling myself:*
> *It'll end someday, somehow.*
> *But I am not sure*
> *I meant what I said.*
>
> *Our love is beautiful,*
> *Filled with pure love.*
> *How can I let it go?*
> *How can I*
> *When I know I have to*
> *Someday, somehow?*

10-13-85

Saw him yesterday at MSD. Great seeing him, but we weren't able to talk much. He is coming on Tuesday and will take me out to lunch. I can't wait. I'm helping some kids with Playboy Nite (our homecoming dance) tonight. I just need to keep myself busy until Tuesday. I hope we will be able to spend several hours together.

10-14-85

I'll see him tomorrow! We haven't really hugged since September 29. Sixteen days now. Yet it feels like months. I need to keep myself busy to kill time. Hopefully, time will go fast. But tomorrow, Lord, please make it slow. I want to be with him as long as possible.

10-17-85

Wonderful, fantastic, great, terrific seeing him two days ago. I almost cried when he had to leave. Love isn't fair sometimes. If we love each other, then why did he have to leave? I know. I understand. He had to leave because it was getting late, 8:30 p.m., but I just didn't want him to leave.

There's a Sadie Hawkins event. I asked a boy named Jay and he accepted. It's the day when the girls have to pay everything.

He is going to call at 11:00 a.m. today to find out the result of my basketball tryouts. But since results won't be posted until tomorrow, I think it's best that I don't answer his call. I want to talk to him but since he isn't supposed to call from school, I'd better not answer.

The janitor just rang our door to let me know I had missed my boyfriend's call. Bridgetta was in the room and she looked at me puzzled. I just laughed and told her janitor was being funny.

10-18-85

> *Love shared by us two*
>> *Has taught me a lot of things*
> *Without our love,*
>> *I probably would never experience anything so*
>> *wonderful.*
>
> *Will I ever give you up?*
>> *Just because of people and family?*
> *Right now, the answer is no!*
>> *I'm selfish – you are mine!*
> *But what will I do in the future?*
>> *Will my mind change?*
>
> *I love you now*
>> *Like I always did*
> *And always will.*

10-21-85

Eight months today since our first kiss. I wanted to call him but did not. I can't charge another bill to Mom and Dad. Wouldn't be a good idea. Tiffany was telling me about her weekend with her boyfriend. I wanted to cry. What about me? Don't I have the right to spend the weekend with him?

Later that same day, I decided to call him. And I cried so hard. Not fair! He isn't there when I need him. We can't be together whenever we want to. Why did I fall in love with him in the first place?

Seeing others being able to hold hands, talk, hug, and kiss freely HURTS! I might as well sleep. It will help kill my time until he calls tomorrow.

10-23-85

I want to quit basketball. I'm tired of all the running. I'm just worn out. I'm always feeling so tired.

10-24-85

He called!!! He is coming on Saturday for the home-coming game, but with his family. Oh well. I haven't gone home since October 6th.

Homecoming Day

He hugged me and kissed me on the cheek. We didn't talk much. I just couldn't. I wonder if his wife knows. I'm just being paranoid, I'm sure. I acted as if he meant nothing. I just talked briefly and as I walked away, he said, "As ever" (our code for "I love you"). I looked at him and said nothing. He then gave me a pleading look. Before I walked away, I made a "peace" sign (meaning "me too").

It's just so **** hard for me to act as if everything is going great. I'm totally opposite of what people think. I'm not as happy as I appear to be.

Most students have gone to Playboy Nite. I hate when people say, "You are not going? Why?" or "You should go" when they talk about different events happening here. I went to Georgetown instead with few students. Ate a Gyro and ice cream. Nothing exciting.

10-28-85

Just done with my aerobics class. I have no motivation to do things like that anymore. I want to get out of here. But where can I go?

10-30-85

He called yesterday and I was upset because we couldn't talk long. I called him right back to apologize, using a made-up number to be billed. I'm not sure why I was upset in the first place. I feel great today. After his call, I got his three letters yesterday and two today. He might come this Saturday if he can come up with an excuse.

11-7-85

Last Monday I sent him a card telling him I wanted to end it all. No letter on Tuesday and yesterday, and I became depressed. So I called him today. His getting my card hurt him so much and it hurts me. I cried. Later, he cried too (that's what he said). I hope to see him this weekend. We need to talk to clear things up. I do love him so much.

11-10-85

We met at the river yesterday. So good to be with him. I'm not going to leave him. I know I told him I wanted to, but now I just couldn't. He said he wanted me to enjoy my college days. He also said he does not want me to regret one day being with him. I don't think I'll ever regret them.

Seeing others fool around, drink, talk nonsense, I can't believe how immature they are – all the kid stuff. I wonder why I'm so different.

My chest is bothering me. It's not painful but it feels funny. When I bend over, it hurts.

11-13-85

I feel sick. Just ate ten cookies this morning. Almost a dozen! I've been lying to everyone saying I have friends. I don't think I have any. In my spare time, I always spend time in this room, my bedroom. What kind of life is that?

Got two letters from him today. Makes me miss him even more, but also makes me realize how great he is. But I really don't know if I should continue our relationship. He said I need to do what is best for me. If only he was younger and wasn't a father.

11-18-85

Something is missing in my life and I don't even know what it is. Who am I? What am I? What do I want? I just don't know. Loneliness just overwhelms me.

I keep eating junk food and just can't stop. I went home Saturday and returned last night. In between, I had eaten five slices of pumpkin pie within thirty-six hours. Gross, isn't it?

Haven't seen him since the 9th. Nine days now.

Later that same day, I just ate more Oreo cookies. Then I vomited.

11-19-85

I feel so down today. We had a scrimmage and I made a lot of mistakes. Coach was mad at me and she criticized me the whole time. Every time she did, I held back my tears. I got F on my test. 59 percent. My first time. I didn't get his letter today.

11-20-85

Got his letter. He said he had been sick.

Chapter 28

November 1985

*H*e and I would call each other twice weekly, same day, same time. I would stand by the pay phone on my dorm floor, my hand on the handset, waiting for it to vibrate. After several weeks, the janitor caught on to our routine and would inform me when the phone rang. But today, I decided to call him during his prep time without notice.

Me: I know we talked yesterday but wanted to call you. How are you feeling now? GA

Him: A little better today. The secretary told me this was Debbie Miller. Am I confused or what? GA

Me: Ha ha. Am I calling at the wrong time?

Him: No way. Nice talking to you.

Me: Great. Oh OK. I'll have a game in three hours. Called Lorraine and she said she will come with BK.

Him: Boy are they lucky. Wish I could. I got a letter from you today, the one you typed in six minutes. Fast typing but many mistakes.

Me: Ha ha. Yeah, sorry about your not coming. But what's more, you are not totally better, so you wouldn't have come anyway.

Him: Yeah, like I said before, I'll wait until I'm told that it is okay to watch the star in action.

Me: I'm not a star. OK, now I'm telling you that you can come and watch, but not tonight OK?

Him: Rules, rules. My, my, what am I to do with you and all the rules you give me? Ha ha.

Me: Sorry. OK, I'll not do that again.

Him: Hope you are smiling??

Me: I'm half-smiling. Oh OK . . . well, as ever!!!

Him: At least you remembered. Ha ha!

Me: Yeah. Well, you'll get a letter this Monday and it will be a depressing one.

Him: It will have to wait till Monday??

Me: Yeah, because I sent it this morning, so the mail won't get in. Unless . . . do you mean why don't I tell you now?

Him: No. I just misunderstood you, that's all. Are you feeling down? Your letter yesterday was very good. Did you get my multicolored letter yet??

Me: Yeah, I'm feeling down. That's why I'm calling you now. Yeah I got your letter today. Great.

Him: Did it help?

Me: A little, but it's not because your letter isn't good. It's just me, that's all.

Him: Okay. I mailed you a short one I wrote really late last night. I shouldn't have stayed up so late, but I had a lot to do. When I take a day off for whatever reason, personal or sick leave or whatever, it seems as if the teacher aides do not know how to follow through with my lesson plans. Oh well . . . so be it. I guess I just wrote you a short one. Sorry, I still love you.

Me: You don't have to say sorry. I've never asked you to write me long letters or to write every day, so getting one letter a week is better than nothing. Ha.

Him: You know I can't do that, right??

Me: I guess so, and I can't do that either.

Him: Kathy told me that you are dating or are being chased by Mike. Not sure if she was testing me or what, so I just went along with it.

Me: BK must have told Kathy. You see, Lorraine wanted to take me out to dinner after the game tonight, and I told her I couldn't because tonight is a Sadie Hawkins night so I'll be gone. Then she asked who was going with me, and I told her just a so-so boy named Jay.

Him: Jay?? Anyway, no problem. I trust you . . . yeah, never a problem. We solved that a long time ago, right?

Me: Yes, but, oh well . . . yeah, his name is Jay, but I'm telling you I don't want to go out tonight. I can't cancel it last minute.

Him: True. Just have fun for yourself. Please just have fun. I miss you and feel the same way often. I told you several times we are very much alike, but don't worry. You really do sound down. Wish I could give you a hug to make the skies blue again.

Me: Yes, I wish too. Oh well. Yeah I'm really feeling so down, and I hope I will do OK in the game today. I'm really worn out mentally, I guess.

Him: Just relax and think positive thoughts. I really mean it. It will help you. Please do it. It really will help. Relax and think positive about anything you want. It can be done and you have the skills and brains to do it. It may take practice, but I know you can do it. I know you well enough now, and I believe you can do it.

Me: I can't relax now. I really can't. I don't know what's wrong with me or what I want.

Him: I can understand, but please try for both my sake and your sake. Hey, who is paying for this call? Some made-up number? Ha ha!

Me: No, I'm going to pay for this, but it won't cost as much as it did the last time because I've thought of a clever way.

Him: What is that?

Me: I called your number and told operator it was from the number in Hagerstown and to bill it to my home.

Him: Fine. Hope I don't go to jail with you. Ha ha!

Me: Very funny. I'm laughing now. I really need that. Oh anyway. I'm telling you I probably will be a lot happier in jail than here.

Him: Hey, you, they don't make coed jails, so we are better off like this than with either you or me in jail. Don't talk like that. You'll depress me; then both of us will end up crying all night. Ha ha!

Me: Ha ha. Oh well, I'm sure you'll never be depressed enough to cry all the night, but it can happen to me.

Him: I can be depressed really bad sometimes but I do as I told you – relax and think positive thoughts. It really works. I do love you very much.

Me: I'm glad. I wish I could think positive, but it seems as if I can't. I can pretend things are going well, but inside it's not.

Him: I know. Hey, congrats on the exam. I was really worried cause you never seem to study.

Me: Yes, I know, and now I'm worried about the research paper. Oh well, like I said in the letter, I'll have it done somehow.

Him: Lord, I hope so. I don't want to date a dummy.

Me: Then don't date a dummy.

Him: I really hope you said that with a big, big smile.

Me: In fact, I wasn't smiling.

Him: Are you trying to tell me something??

Me: Maybe, but the problem is that I don't know about myself anymore or why I am feeling whatever I'm feeling. Just simply . . . I don't know!

Him: Okay, I understand and won't pressure you anymore. I just want you to be okay and to get things straight in your own mind without pressure from me. I told you before, nothing can change how I feel about you. I'll just have to wait until you get things together. I'm just sad that I can't be there to look at you, as I always make you nervous. I do care, and right now you are more important than anything in my life and I want you to feel good about yourself, about me, and about us. And you, you, you come first. You have to come first because Debbie has to live with Debbie first and see her in the mirror every day. Everything else comes second. I just wish I could help. I feel so helpless. I told you two weeks ago I see you as drowning or slipping from me and I can't seem to stop you, but I understand how you feel and I know it is not easy for you. Please don't feel guilty if you want me to back off and leave you alone for a while. Please let me know. I do care about you and respect you.

Me: I know you care and I'm not feeling guilty or whatever. My feeling so low isn't because of you; it's because of something I'm not even sure of. Without you it might be worse. I dunno, but seems that the only time I'm happy is when I'm with you or when I'm at home. I want to know what is bothering me, and it bothers me to know that I don't know. I cried all night last night. I was in Tiffany's room by then, and I don't know why I cried. Partly it was because I would 100 percent prefer to eat out with Lorraine and BK instead of going with Jay tonight, but it's a little thing and yet I cried. Why???? I don't know. Seems like everything isn't going right for me, and sometimes I just want to cry for no reason. What is happening to me???? That was why I said I hope I would do good at the game tonight. It's because right now I don't feel good and I don't know if I could play. Even worse, Lorraine and BK will be here. If they will not be there, then I don't give a **** if I do lousy tonight.

Him: Hey, you won't do lousy. I'm sure of that, and

I'm not trying to cheer you up. I'm sure of it. It sounds as if I am a heavy weight on your mind and I just seem to bother you, or it's our relationship and the fact that we hide so much and sneak around that really must be bothering you. I'm so sorry for hurting you. I'm really sorry but still I love you and that will never change. Maybe you need a break from the sneaking to see if it is me. Lord, I hate to say that; it was really hard, but I hate to see you in such bad shape. I love you too much for that.

Me: Is it because of you?? I don't know. I honestly don't know. Seems that I cry over little things that I used to not cry over. I'm tired of the life I'm living now. I'm just tired of it, and I told Tiffany last night I wish I could just die! Oh well. I think I better close for now. We have talked for more than thirty minutes I think.

Him: Thirty-eight to be exact. I don't know either, but it sounds like pressure, and if it is, then it is my fault. Also, dying is not the answer. Please believe me, that is not the answer. I better close, but I hate to end on a negative note. I feel you can get through. Please try to cheer up.

Me: You've never died before, so you can't say it isn't the answer. (But don't worry, I won't do anything to harm myself.) Oh well, I hope I won't look that bad, I'm crying now, and hope I'll look as if everything is fine. Oh well, yes, I have to go now. I'm glad I called you though. I just wish I could see you. I miss you terribly. I love you. (I'm ending on a positive note. Ha.)

Him: Good! I'm glad you called too. I love you too

and will no matter what. I miss you just as much as you miss me. Please don't cry. I can't stand the taste of tears when we kiss. Ha ha. I love you. GA to SK

Me: OK. SK

Him: As ever. SK

Me: As ever. SK

Chapter 29

Winter 1985

*P*aper had always been my friend and confidant. But, now, I found myself revisiting my journal entries, memorizing my writing, the lines pulling me further into depression and misery. I think that was one of the reasons my journaling eventually ceased.

12-03-85

So cold outside. Winter is here, at least I think so. Like always, I end up some days feeling like crying. Today is one of those days. Last night, Bridgetta said maybe I should drink in order to make friends. No way! Maybe I don't drink because of childhood memories. I remember Dad came home drunk one night. I was so disgusted with him. Just once; is it possible that my experience had such a strong impression on me?

12-05-85

Two more weeks until I go home. He called twice, at 11:30 a.m. and 10:30 p.m. I have a written evaluation I must pass in order to pass English. He said writing letters and essays are the same. To me they aren't. Whenever I have to write, my mind gets blocked. I don't write as freely as I do when I write letters. He said my grammar is great. Is that so?

12-06-85

I was supposed to get his four-page letter today, but I didn't. Very depressing! Post Office is slow sometimes. My chest feels as if something is inside, so thick that it's hard to breathe. I can breathe, but I can feel something tight inside. It has been bothering me for some time. Not sure if I should have it checked.

I've been gaining weight. Here's what I had for breakfast: OJ, milk, omelet, ham, two English muffins, cereal, and a blueberry muffin. For lunch, I had three slices of tomatoes, an apple, and ice cream with peanut butter.

12-08-85

Such a beautiful day. I wanted to go out for a walk or ride a bike, but there is no one I can ask to go with me. I'm all alone in my room, doing nothing much. I started crocheting but didn't have a clue as to what I wanted to make.

I wrote him a letter but think I'll just throw it away. Boring and lonely here.

12-09-85

My heart twisting
  My eyes blinking
Trying to hold back tears
  Aching everywhere
Wanting to be free
  Wanting to laugh
Wanting to have a friend
  Yet I'm not free from those feelings

I'm crying
  Instead of laughing
I have no one to talk to,
    To laugh with,
  To hold,
    And to share.

12-12-85

Ironed my shirt today while daydreaming about him and us. I ended up burning my shirt. Ugh. He called today. There wasn't much for us to talk about. I'm not sure how I feel. Should I just end it?

12-16-85

Almost cried this afternoon after I called home. I wanted to have the car this week but Mom said I couldn't. Looks like I won't be able to go home until Friday. **** this world! I just want to go home.

12-20-85

Gave him two gifts. Coffee mug and a sweater. I really hope he likes it and that the sweater fits him.

He called before I saw him. **** hard! I love him. At times I just don't realize how much. Wish I could see him tomorrow. We had planned to meet, but then Mom said she had to use the car. She ended up not needing the car.

Christmas Day

I'm crying now. I cried last year as well. Last year, it

was because of David. Today, it's because of every-thing. We had to visit our relatives. I didn't want to go but Grandma insisted. Why can't she understand? What will I do there? Just sit and pretend I'm enjoying myself while everyone talks?

Today is supposed to be the day we celebrate the birth of Jesus and look at me. I am crying.

12-28-85

Called him yesterday. He won't be able to get away tomorrow. He has to take his son and some of his friends to Children's Hospital to visit a girl.

I'm having mixed feelings about everything. My call to him wasn't what I wanted. Yes, we talked but it's always when, where, how, and what time to meet.

I want to end it all, but when I tell him I end up feel-ing like crying. It would probably be best if I did, but I don't think I could go on through second semester without him. Nobody realizes I have no friends. None! I'm telling you, none!

12-30-85

I wonder if Mom suspects because I think I talk about him a lot. Maybe I'm just being paranoid.

2-22-86

Just called him an hour ago and I feel great. A feeling of contentment having talked to him. I ended our rela-tionship a month and two days ago, but when we met last week we did just the same thing.

Chapter 30

"Let me introduce to you Mr and Mrs Peter Myers," Peter's best man and brother, Jeff, announced as we stepped into the reception room. Immediately, everyone stood; half of them held up their arms straight into the air, waving their hands, while the other half clapped. Those who clapped quickly caught on to the Deaf way to applaud.

Peter and I held hands as we walked over to the long head table and took our seats. The wedding party was seated in one row; groomsmen on the left and bridesmaids on the right. In front of us were round tables filled with our guests. We had a good view of everyone: relatives (mostly from my side), Mom and Dad's friends, high school classmates, and a very few of Peter's friends from college.

As soon as we seated ourselves, the guests at the Deaf table began swirling their cloth napkins in the air.

Peter and I looked at each other and smiled, knowing that this ritual would continue throughout the night. We exchanged a kiss, a brief yet tender one.

The napkins immediately went up in the air again, waving wildly. Apparently, the kiss they had witnessed was not enough. They wanted more. A show, perhaps. This time, Peter pulled me up from my chair, draped his left arm around my back, held my head with his right hand and bent me backward. His face met mine and he kissed me, this time more passionately. Everyone cheered and returned to their conversations among themselves.

It was my special day, yet in the back of my mind, I was

worried. I was aware of how difficult the day must have been for *him*. I also felt bad for all the kissing he had to witness.

Guilt is such a burden. It can cripple us. I felt responsible for what had happened, and I'd need a little over ten years to finally let go of the guilt.

Chapter 31

Fall 1986 – Sophomore Year

I had survived my freshman year. I found myself once again packing my belongings for another year at Gallaudet. Mom and Dad knew nothing about my unhappiness. They did not question my reasons for coming home frequently. To satisfy any curiosity, though, I simply told them that I didn't drink, smoke, or party, which was true. Of course, they didn't know the other reason.

During my sophomore year I felt numb and disconnected from everything.

I did not cry much.

I did not keep a journal.

I did not participate in any campus activities.

I gave up playing basketball, my favorite sport.

I ate my meals alone, showing up at the cafeteria during the nonpeak hours.

I sat in the library by the window during the day, watching everyone pass by.

I lived for Fridays. I would meet him on my way home, always planning around his schedule. We would meet at the park-and-ride for our hour together.

I dreaded Sundays. I would return to school late into the night, already counting the days until Friday.

I allowed my grades to drop. The first year, I had maintained a 3.31 cumulative grade point average. My second year, my GPA dropped to an unspectacular 3.0.

I remember *nothing* about that year except for my daily trips to the local convenience store.

How could a person so popular and carefree have fallen into a bottomless pit in just a few years? I was more isolated than I ever thought possible.

Chapter 32

Fall 1986 – Spring 1987

I walked across the campus to the parking lot where my car was parked. With a car of my own, an older-model Buick my great-uncle had passed on to me, I could now go off campus as I pleased. I got in the car and decided to drive around DC for a while before parking at my usual spot by the High's.

It was still early when I pulled into "my" spot. It was 7:45 p.m. and the sky had begun to get dark. The darker, the better; Gallaudet students wouldn't recognize me if they happened to come by the store. When they did, I would make sure I sat low in my seat or kept my head down, pretending to be doing something. I looked at my watch; it was only 8:03 p.m. and it was going to be a very long night. I usually remained at High's until late into the night, 9:30 p.m. or so, before returning to campus. I would then slip into my room, pretending I had been out having a good time.

Sometimes I would bring something to read, usually a magazine, or work on my homework assignments to help pass the time. Other times, I would observe people as they walked in and out of High's, always interesting to look at. More often than not, I found myself wondering about life and fantasizing about death.

. . . I got out of the car, not paying attention, when a car sped by, hitting me. I flew into the air, my head hitting the curb as I landed on the pavement several feet away. People came running to me, shouting: "Someone call 911." I was bleeding badly when the paramedics arrived, trying to rescue me. It was too late. A sheet covered my body and face as they wheeled me into the ambulance.

. . . I was in High's looking for something sweet to eat when everyone shouted, "Get down." I didn't hear them, and as I pulled out a pint of my favorite ice cream from the freezer I felt something sharp hit my chest. I had been shot. I collapsed on the floor. After the masked guy fled, the customers screamed: "Someone help her."

. . . Mom and Dad opened their front door and realized something was wrong. The gentlemen had solemn expressions on their faces when they asked: "Is your daughter Debbie Anderson?" Mom had replied: "Yes." The visitors then said: "We're sorry to tell you this, but your daughter has been killed."

. . . People stood in the long line, patiently waiting their turn to see me in a coffin: My family. My relatives. Mom and Dad's friends. My high school friends. And everyone who knew me from MSD (teachers, coaches, and staff). Everyone moved slowly. When they reached the coffin, they commented, "She was a sweet girl." "She didn't deserve to die like this." And "I wish I had gotten to know her better."

How I wished I could die. How peaceful that would be. There would be no more tears. No more pain either. I certainly wanted to die, but I couldn't kill myself. Not because I was scared, but because that would be a sign of weakness.

Weakness was something Mom mocked and perhaps even despised. If I committed suicide, that would imply I was weak and not strong enough to make it through life. As strange as it may sound, it also meant that Mom would win. And there was no way I was going to let her do that.

Chapter 33

April 1987

I stared at the paper posted on the wall. Had I read it correctly? I placed my finger on the line where my name was spelled out and slid my finger toward the right, where my internship site was listed. Next to my name was *S.C.H.I., TX.* What was going on? It had to be a mistake.

I had applied for several summer internships – two in Washington, DC, and a few others I couldn't remember. I really didn't care as long as I could get out of here and keep myself busy for the summer.

I walked into my internship placement counselor's office. The minute she saw me, she said, "Congratulations."

"There is a mistake with my internship," I said.

"What mistake?" She flipped through her papers until she found my information. "Your internship is at Southwest Center for the Hearing Impaired."

"Right. Here in DC. The paper says Texas."

"No," she said looking at the paper. "It's actually in Texas."

"Remember, I applied to two places in DC," I reminded her. We had met several weeks earlier to discuss potential internship sites.

"That's right, you did. You also applied to several others."

"I know. But my phone conversation last week was with the agency in DC."

"The agency you applied to is located in the southwest section of DC. They didn't offer you an internship. The phone conversation you had last week was with Southwest Center for the Hearing Impaired," she explained.

Then she suddenly figured out my confusion. "The word *southwest* must have gotten you mixed up," she said.

Yes, I had mixed up the two places. I slowly sank into the chair. "So, I'm going to *Texas?*" I asked feebly.

"Yes." She looked at me, a bit worried. "Is that okay? You had already told them you would take the job."

That explained the interviewer's first question as I replayed our phone conversation in my head. After introducing ourselves, the interviewer had asked if I was from Texas. I remember thinking what an odd question that was. But, I let it pass as he proceeded with more questions. In the end, he asked if I would like to accept the internship, and I said yes.

I walked out of the office dazed. I only had a few weeks before the semester was over, and I was supposed to begin my internship the first week of June. A plane reservation had to be made. What would Mom and Dad say? Texas was so far away. Would I be able to handle not seeing *him* for two months? So many questions filled my mind.

I had tried to escape the summer before. I had accepted an internship at Camp Harold F. Whittle in Fawnskin, California. Unfortunately, it was one of the loneliest times in my life. I didn't realize I would be the only Deaf person on the staff; there was one other intern who was deaf, but she was not culturally Deaf. Besides, she was placed at another site of the camp. When I had considered the internship, I was told I would be working with a group of deaf campers, but when I arrived I learned that the deaf campers wouldn't arrive until the end of the summer.

After barely two weeks at the camp, loneliness overwhelmed me, and I couldn't handle it. My year at Gallaudet had been better than this; at least I had full access to communication.

Tension at home had been better than this. My limited time with him had been better than this.

I wanted to go home. My dilemma: I had no money to purchase a one-way return ticket. I couldn't ask Mom or Dad; they wouldn't have the money. In desperation, I called *him,* hoping he would be able to rescue me. He did.

After announcing the news to Mom and Dad about my summer plans in San Antonio, Mom was skeptical. "You won't stay. You will want to come home. Remember last year," she said with a smirk.

Perhaps she was right. I didn't know. What I did know was that I needed to leave – Gallaudet, home, and him.

Chapter 34

April 1987

I sat in the car, waiting. He was supposed to meet me at 4:00 p.m., and it was a few minutes past. Our time together was always short, and I wanted him to hurry so that we could have as much time as possible together. As soon as I saw his car approaching, my heart quickened. When he pulled into a parking spot, I jumped out of the car and waited for him to walk over. We each took a quick glance around our surroundings to ensure that nobody was watching before getting into the backseat of my car.

Like always, we shut the door and fell into each other's arms – each of us holding on for dear life. In his arms, I felt so safe and loved. And then, my head resting on his shoulder, I looked up to him and said: "I want you to make love to me."

He looked at me in surprise. "Are you sure?" he asked. We had talked about it in the past but had never crossed the line. I was a virgin and had every intention of remaining one until I was married. But, today, I had a different plan.

"Yes, I'd like for you to make love to me," I repeated.

"There's nothing more I'd want in this world than to make love to you. I'd be honored."

"Then, let's do it," I said.

He cupped my face in his hand and kissed me tenderly. He then looked into my eyes and shook his head. "Not in the car. You deserve better than that," he said.

Unbeknownst to him, I had made plans.

I was going to leave him this time, for good. I knew, I thought, that I would never find anyone else, or get married, for that matter. So, because I was leaving him, I wanted my virginity to be taken by someone I loved; a sweet memory I would hold dearly in my heart.

I was also hoping against all odds that I would get pregnant. I would then remain in Texas after the internship to raise our child alone. He needn't know. He had a family of his own. With our child, I would have a part of him with me always.

The thought of leaving him was so very difficult; when I thought about it, I wept. But I knew one thing for certain, I just couldn't go on living this way. The hiding and sneaking had taken its toll on me. Knowing he had a wife to go home to every time we departed confused me. I understood his need to keep his family together for the sake of his children who were a few years younger than me. But if he really loved me, how could a few extra minutes spent with me hurt his children? If he would rather be with me than with his wife, why couldn't he find the excuses necessary to stay a bit longer?

My eyes swelled with tears, as always, as the time approached for him to go home. Our last few minutes together were spent in each other's arms. I cried, and he tried to comfort me, telling me not to cry, and that he would try to stay a bit longer the next time we saw each other. Then, it was time for him to leave.

But not before we made plans to meet – at his home.

Chapter 35

O ur two-tier wedding cake was not supposed to look the way it did.

I couldn't remember when we had checked on the cake. Was it the night before, or a few hours before our wedding? But when we did, I was horrified. "This is not what I ordered," I said. Had Peter misunderstood me when we placed an order? He was the one who voiced for me, after all.

The Italian baker, who was also the owner, had added his own touches without my permission – blue frosted flowers on the top of the cake. I wanted to tell him to scrape off the frosting and do the job all over again.

"Let's just forget it," Peter said. "It isn't that bad, really." I thought the baker's touches ruined everything but decided to let it go.

On the top we had placed a wedding figurine that Mom and Dad had used on their wedding cake. People commented on the antique when they saw it. As people gathered around the cake to witness its cutting, I immediately noticed something was missing.

"K-n-i-f-e," I fingerspelled, low enough so no one except Peter could see. Peter was clueless. "Knife," I repeated. "Where is it?"

Peter whispered to a wedding attendee in the reception room and a knife was brought in. A plain standard piece of silverware from the same set with which everyone had eaten during our reception. That was not the knife I was referring to. The wedding knife that I had purchased was nowhere to be found.

We had no choice but to proceed with our agenda. We cut the cake in two slices and placed them on two napkins that read: THIS IS THE DAY I WILL MARRY MY FRIEND.

Holding the cake on a napkin in my left hand, I looked at Peter mischievously. "Ready?" I asked. Peter glanced at me, not trusting me. How I loved to tease.

In a slow motion, we brought cake toward each other, not trusting what one would do to the other. As soon as Peter opened his mouth to receive the cake, I smeared it all over his mouth. He returned the gesture.

And we laughed so hard.

Everyone raved about the cake after they were served. Inside was a rum filling the baker had promised would delight everyone.

"Rum?" I had asked when we discussed our order. I didn't drink and didn't want alcohol served during our wedding.

"You can't taste it," the baker had assured me.

"The alcohol will evaporate when it is being baked," Peter explained.

"Trust me, everyone raves about this filling," the baker added. "You won't be disappointed."

But I was.

Oddly, when it came to the cake, misfortunes continued. First, it was the extra touches to the icing. Then, the wedding knife was missing. And despite the ravings, I didn't like the rum filling. Finally, several weeks later, the professional photographer regretfully informed us that the pictures of our cake exchange didn't come through. Go figure.

Disappointments happen. Misfortunes occur. Life has its share of adversity, but, as long as we have true joy, they cannot dampen our spirit.

Chapter 36

My car slowed down as I turned onto his street. I knew where he lived. I knew what his house looked like. Directions were not needed. I had driven by his house once secretly just to get a glimpse.

It was mid-morning. His wife was at work. His children were at school. He would be going to work later that day. We didn't have much time.

As I pulled into his driveway, I looked around to make sure nobody was outside. I didn't want his neighbors to see me walk into the house. Turning the engine off, I paused for several seconds. It was now or never. After I got out of the car, I walked up to the front of his house and rang the doorbell.

He opened the door immediately.

"Are you sure you want to?" he asked the moment I stepped into his house.

"Yes." I was determined to follow through.

Holding my hand, he led me through the hall toward his bedroom. I took in all the sights: Pictures of his children. The color of the painting on the wall. The bed where he slept with her every night. His personal belongings alongside hers on the dresser. And just about everything else I could lay my eyes on.

What I had envisioned as a beautiful, memorable moment was shattered. Our lovemaking had barely begun when it ended abruptly.

"I'm so sorry," he apologized afterward. "I couldn't contain myself. I was just too excited. I hope it was worth it."

"It's okay," I reassured him. "I enjoyed it." I lied. What else could I have said?

As I drove away, I thought, *So that was it? Why do people have such a preoccupation with sex?*

Chapter 37

June 1987

My return ticket was for August. There was no turning back.

Our plane flew out of Baltimore Washington International airport. My head rested against the window pane as I looked down, my eyes glued to the beautiful design of the land that came into view as we ascended, multiple shades of green laid out in a quilt-pattern slowly disappearing the higher we flew.

We had a four-hour layover in Atlanta because of heavy rainstorms. I was tired and hungry when we finally landed in San Antonio around midnight. Not many people were around because of the hour, and I easily spotted a stranger holding a sign that spelled out s.c.h.i. in large letters. As we proceeded to the baggage claim, I was told my suitcase had been misplaced. The following morning, I awoke groggily in the same clothes in which I had traveled. *What a great way to begin my summer,* I thought.

I had business to take care of, and it wasn't long before I found the front office. The Southwest Center for the Hearing Impaired (SCHI) was a nonprofit organization providing life-adjustment and employment skills training for Deaf adults. I was hired to coordinate recreational activities within its residential program. When I stepped inside the office, I was greeted warmly by a handsome man. He was tanned and athletic looking. A tail of hair ran down back of his neck, about two inches long, and he wore a silver earring in his left ear. Around his neck was a silver necklace, which matched a smaller version around his wrist – not a style I was used to seeing.

"Good morning," he said with a smile. "I'm Peter. You must be Deb." After asking how my flight was, he rambled on: "I was so disappointed I had to leave the airport at eleven last night before you arrived. I had to get back for my night shift."

I returned his smile. "We had a long delay, but I'm glad to be here finally. Actually, I'm here to see if I could borrow the phone. I need to call Southwest to see if they have located my suitcase," I said, self-conscious of how rumpled my clothes looked.

"I can call for you," he offered. We made small talk. I learned that he had recently been accepted into Gallaudet's graduate program and would be going in the fall.

"I'd love to get together with you sometime soon. I have so many questions about Gallaudet, if you don't mind." He smiled.

I had determined to leave Gallaudet behind for the summer but found myself saying, "Sure."

Chapter 38

June 1987

$\mathcal{T}$rue to his word, Peter asked me out several days later. We went to Maggie's café and spent the next two hours eating and talking about Gallaudet.

After our first "date," he asked me out again. We sampled goat-milk fudge at a Mexican market, went window shopping at North Star Mall, ate chicken fried steak at the I-10 Diner, and finished with cookies at Fuddrucker's. Our five-hour outing was pleasant; I found him easy to talk to, and I had a good time. After that we visited the San Antonio Zoo. We strolled along the River Walk. We dined at a variety of restaurants. We sunbathed in Port Aransas.

Peter was the perfect excuse for my break up with *him*. Two weeks after I set foot in Texas, I wrote him a letter and told him that I had met someone else. And that it was over between the two of us. There was some truth to it. I had met Peter, but he did not need to know we were not romantically involved.

Soon the clients and staff at SCHI took notice and teased me about Peter and I liking each other. I brushed them off, saying Peter just wanted to show me around San Antonio. In truth, we were spending more and more time together during our after-work hours. Unknown to most, I also spent many nights keeping Peter company when he worked third shift. After the clients went to bed, we often played pool and talked late into early morning hours.

We talked about a lot of things, including my affair.

Six weeks into the summer, Peter wrote me a letter.

Deb,

Just wanted to let you know that I was thinking about you. You seem to be on my mind constantly lately – gee, I wonder why!?

Since you walked into my life, things have been so bright. I was really having a hard time with work, dealing with leaving Texas, and my attitude and feelings in general. Suddenly, you show up and everything begins to change. Thanks!

It's been so long since I could trust someone to talk about anything, without fear of their reaction. I feel so comfortable with you. I don't think there is anything I wouldn't tell you. That's strange and new for me. Exciting too.

My history with relationships has not been that great. I don't want sympathy, but I feel as though I was mistreated. I gave and gave and got nothing in return. With you, I feel a genuine concern from you with regard to my feelings, emotions, and thoughts. Thank you for making me feel so *wonderful!!!*

My feelings toward you continue to grow. I never thought I'd feel this way about any person again. I must admit that I'm somewhat scared about it all. (Don't worry, you could *never* scare me away.) I guess it's the newness. Anyway, I do worry about you and your situation (past) and hope you know I'm here whenever you need me. Thank you for being in my life.

Love, Peter

Unlike my experience at Gallaudet where I was alone, I was now having the time of my life. I was well-liked by both the clients and staff, and my schedule was never dull. As a recreation coordinator intern, I implemented activities for our clients. A pool tournament was set up. I taught female clients how to crotchet. I participated in the male baseball team as a manager. I was one of the chaperones, taking clients to Laredo, Mexico.

The staff included me in their activities after work hours as well: shopping, cookouts, horseback riding, movies at a drive-in, sightseeing, and tubing.

No one knew about my past. No one would have guessed. My pain was swept aside – for the time being.

Chapter 39

August 1987 – Junior Year

$\mathcal{I}$nstead of flying back home, I decided to hitch a ride back to Gallaudet with Peter. With all the stuff he had to bring to school in his small Volkswagen Rabbit, I just managed to fit into the front seat. We traveled east through Louisiana, sightseeing in New Orleans and sunbathing at Panama City Beach, Florida, before traveling north.

A week before our departure from SCHI, Peter had given me a card, in which he wrote: "Maybe it's my imagination, but I've felt strange 'vibrations' or feelings between us. I hope everything is alright – if not, I'd love to talk about it." He had read me correctly. As my internship came to an end, I began to feel uneasy. I didn't want to return home. I didn't want to go back to Gallaudet. It was difficult for me to accept that my summer had come to an end. And to know what was waiting for me – a return to lifelessness at Gallaudet – was unbearable. To make matters worse, I wasn't even sure where my relationship with Peter was going.

After six days on the road, the Welcome to Maryland sign came into view. I started to feel nauseated, and as soon as I saw the sign for my hometown, Williamsport, I broke down into tears. "I don't want to go home," I said. My summer had been surreal and I was not ready to face reality. So we delayed our arrival by checking into a motel room. After Peter and I went to a nearby convenience store for chocolate chip cookies and milk, we spent the rest of the night talking.

Peter spent the first two days visiting my family before he

left for Gallaudet to attend the New Student Orientation. The following day, I met *him* at a restaurant near my home. We sat in the booth and talked. He cried the whole time. We parted, and I lingered in Dad's car long after he drove off. I don't remember how I felt. He called later, leaving a message, asking if he could see me. So we met again, five days later. I have no recollection of what took place that day.

When I returned to Gallaudet, for my junior year, I began to feel angry.

For two and a half years, I had been faithful to him. I had gone out a few times my first semester at Gallaudet, just for the sake of appearances, but did nothing beyond a good night hug. But he was still married.

During my second year at Gallaudet, I grew to distrust my roommate. She was a basketball teammate of mine from my freshman year. How we ended up being roommates, I couldn't remember. From time to time, she would say something like: "Another letter from your secret boyfriend, huh?" Or she would smile knowingly and ask, "What are you reading? A love letter?" I was fearful of jeopardizing his name or career at MSD, so after reading his letters, I would destroy them immediately. The Deaf world was so small that with just a glimpse of his name, the entire Deaf community, from East to West, would know about us. Because of my fear, I avoided being in *my* own bedroom as much as possible. This was another reason why I quit keeping a journal.

I could not develop friendships with anyone. Not even one. And now, after two years alone, it was too late to form new ones. But, what about him? Everything about him had remained the same. Home. Family. Friends. Career. All was well.

Yes, I was angry.

Chapter 40

August 1989

Gifts of various sizes piled up on the floor in Grandma's living room. Peter and I sat on the floor, taking turns opening the gifts as our family members watched.

Halfway through opening, *his* gift landed in my lap. I carefully peeled the tape off the wrapping paper and lifted the item out of a cardboard box. I then held it in the air for everyone to see. It was a small Quartz clock, maybe six inches tall and plated in gold. It was a standard gift, nothing special. Did he pick it out? I doubt it. His wife probably did.

He had given me a present once earlier – a 14-karat gold necklace. Hanging on the necklace was a cursive-letter D with a diamond chip on it. The necklace was presented to me during my senior year of high school, several weeks after our first kiss.

Gifts were not given with joy or excitement in our house. I always felt they were a burden, something that Mom and Dad had to give because everyone else was doing it. My siblings and I were reminded constantly that Mom grew up with no gifts; not even for a birthday or Christmas. In fact, she was twenty-one when she received her first birthday present.

Mom had wanted us to know that her life was more difficult, so we had no room to be ungrateful. When I was fourteen, I did not get a birthday present, and I knew better than to say anything. Mom had promised she would get me a belated gift as soon as she had extra money. But that never happened. I heard the same promise the next several birthdays. Though she made sure my siblings received their gifts, I never complained when I was overlooked. And, if I was given gift money from relatives, I would put it aside knowing Mom and Dad would ask for it later. So to receive a gold necklace from him, an unexpected gift for no special occasion, was something I had cherished.

I wore the necklace every single day except when I played sports. It was so much part of me that I felt bare without it. I had told him I would always wear it, a promise I felt obliged to honor. After all, a promise was a promise. And it was a gift for no reason. Explaining to Peter what the necklace represented would be difficult; I didn't even understand it myself.

Then one day, a week before my engagement to Peter, the necklace broke and fell off. When I noticed it was gone, I realized that it was a blessing to no longer have it around my neck.

I thought Peter was the greatest gift I could have ever received, but he wasn't. There is an even greater gift – the greatest Gift of all.

Chapter 41

September 1987

"How do you define love?" Peter asked.

"What love means to *me?*" I asked, making sure I understood his question.

He nodded. "I'm just curious."

"Love..." Why did he ask me? I felt cornered. "Love means... you accept the person for who she is, you would always be there no matter what. It means..." I stammered. "It means you can be yourself. You feel free; you can share about anything – your feelings, dreams, and fears."

He didn't say anything. So I continued: "Love means you enjoy being with the person." He didn't say anything still, and I felt awkward. "Your turn," I said abruptly.

"You and I think alike," he said, taking my hands in his. Then, letting go of my left hand, he looked at me and said for the first time: "I love you."

And I knew I felt the same. I had fallen in love with him.

Though Peter represented a glimmer of hope, I recognized that my life was a total mess, and I needed help. With his encouragement, I walked into the counseling center at Gallaudet and had my first session on September 21.

Sitting in front of a stranger was indeed awkward, but I knew that I had to make changes. My determination quickly turned into frustration, however. The counselor kept on focusing on the *present.* Never mind my upbringing. The counselor thought I was avoiding the real issues and encouraged me to center on the here and now. She encouraged me to recognize my negative thinking patterns and work on changing the way I think. I disagreed with her approach; I just knew that my past played a significant role in the person I had become. After three or four sessions, I realized that counseling wasn't working; I quit.

I tried very hard to remain optimistic about life in general, but I did not do a good job of it. In one of my letters to Peter, I wrote: "I'm really trying. With your encouraging words, it means a lot. It's a nice feeling, knowing you believe in me. Please don't ever get frustrated if I just cry and feel down. I'll keep on trying. It's going to be *very hard* but I'll try…"

And, I did try. On November 12, Peter gave me a card with eight balloons that spelled out: "G-O-O-D L-U-C-K." On the inside, he wrote: "Deb, I wanted to let you know that I'm behind you 100 percent today. I know you'll do great. I'm really proud of you! I love you, Peter." And, he was my number one fan during the following four months as I returned to the basketball court.

I did well in my classes, ending the semester with As and Bs, and a place on the Dean's List.

However, toward the end of our first semester together, Peter began to see more and more of the "real" me, and he admitted that he wasn't sure he could handle my unhappiness.

My glimmer of hope began to fade.

Chapter 42

November 1987

Peter,

I do love you and I do not think I was looking for excuses when I said, "Maybe I am not good enough for you." Really, if our relationship does not turn out the way you wanted or expected, why stay and suffer? I am not suggesting anything, but I feel that if I do not meet your expectations, I have failed.

Heaven knows, I tried to share everything, but it's so hard. I'm struggling with my inner feelings about everything. At times, I feel defeated and it is as if my efforts do not count and that I just can't do anything right.

Concerning my being incapable of sharing everything, I honestly do not think you understand. How can I suddenly change everything in a few months? Can you, a future counselor, answer that? I grew up accepting things and calmly blaming myself for everything. I shut my mouth when I disagreed. When I was hurt, I pretended it never happened. I never got the opportunity (or at least I never learned how) to do what I wanted or tell what I felt. Instead, I placed everyone else first. I never knew how to express myself except on paper, because no one cared enough to ask (when they did, they criticized my feelings). So, I kept everything to myself and it was as if I never knew how to get mad or let anger surface.

You came, and as much as I wanted you, I knew I had to force myself to change. I improved a little and told you how I felt. It was more than I thought I was capable of doing. I tried to believe you that what I have to say is important. But my doubts would return when you were not attentive to what I had to say, especially when there were distractions, such as the TV, in the background. I believe that my talk is so-so when I share about school, basketball, and my grades. I would appreciate it if you give me your full attention. What bothers me is that you demand to know every detail when you notice something bothering me. What about my general, daily talk? Aren't they equally important?

I guess I have a lot of things I need to change. There, as usual, I always end up blaming myself. So be it. I am hurting for myself and for both of us. It is hard, knowing that my life is all messed up. I keep on telling myself something good will come out of it and I know I'm good, but if you don't have any patience left, just go and leave me alone. I have survived, and I will survive.

I love you but I want you to be happy.

Love,

Deb

* * *

November 30, 1987

Deb,

So much that I want to tell you. I was afraid that if I tried to remember it all, I'd mess it up. Thus the letter.

I thought long and hard this afternoon about what you said, what I did, etc. You really did a brave thing by telling me that "This is me; if you don't like it, leave!" I know these weren't your exact words. It does not matter. I really respect you for taking such a chance and "putting it on the line" with me. It showed me that you have your way of being you, and that I should let you do just that: be you. So what if you don't tell me everything you're thinking and feeling. When, in fact, you do: in your own way. So what if you don't handle things the way I handle things. The point is, you do, but in your own way. I guess I'm trying to say that you have a right to live your life and be you. I am so very sorry for ever expecting anything other than that. You really opened my eyes today as to just how many of your qualities I respect and admire; and you opened my eyes as to how self-centered I was being.

Thank you for being patient with me. You haven't failed at all. You've succeeded in getting it through my thick skull that I can't create a person or a relationship, only participate and do my best with me. A valuable lesson!

Again, I apologize for not being attentive to your needs. To think that I haven't been paying attention to you hurts. The truth hurts though. I will sincerely try to do better. I am easily distracted and have been since I can remember, especially when I'm tired. It's especially noticeable with you and me because we sign. No excuses. I am sorry. You're right; I, too, feel that *everything* you say is important. I need to show it, and I'll try.

I love you, Deb. You make me the *happiest* guy on earth. I could not and will not go and leave you alone. You're stuck with me. Besides, I'd be a real mess without my sweetie by my side.

Yours *always,*

Peter

* * *

Peter,

I came by the dorm at 10:55 p.m. and waited for you. It's now 12:10 a.m. and I *really* wanted to see you, but I don't know what time you'll be back, so I might as well write. The strange thing is that I don't want to write because I want to talk. Just need to get out whatever is inside so that I can sleep peacefully for a few hours tonight.

Please believe me that letting you go is the last thing I would want to do. But, don't you see? I was in a situation where I was more than miserable, and he knew that yet he never let me go. It is something that I suffered and I always wished he could at least agree on letting me go. I was weak because I thought I loved him; in fact, I couldn't tolerate the thought of not having him around. So, I stayed. And look at me – I ended up, suffering just the same.

Now, with you, I hurt to know that it's *me* who caused these problems. What is **** wrong with me? I fight against myself. I fight, trying to change. It's hard. Now, it even hurts more to know that you were miserable all along when you said you were happy. So, naturally, I understood and I felt I had to let you go, because if I don't, later in your life you'll resent me for not doing so. You're wonderful, and God knows how much I love you.

I'm scared to have you out of my life. You're a big part of my life but I'll survive. I've learned that no matter how much I cry or suffer, it won't kill me. So, I'm willing to suffer if it means freedom for you from me. So what if I suffer? I may deserve it, for I'm not being me when I am with you here at Gallaudet. It's what our problem is all about, isn't it?

It really hurts. If you chose to doubt that, I don't care. I'm the only one who knows exactly how I feel. I care, but what I mean is that people are entitled to their own feelings and opinions.

I struggle to be normal; I thought I succeeded in the beginning, but for some reason, I don't know, it went down the drain. I've told you before we came that I hate it here. It's hard to go on when it's as if everything is pushing me down, smashing me into pieces. How do I get up and smile?

At first, when you told me what you were feeling, I panicked. I thought I lost you for good. Then you said you didn't know what you wanted to do. Relief washed over me and I felt optimistic. But then you said you couldn't handle my unhappiness. What was

I supposed to say? "Don't worry I'll try to be happy next semester?" It would have been an enormous lie. I can't guarantee I'll ever change when I'm here. So, it's *unfair* to you if I want us to work at it. You know, deep inside your heart, that I have failed. So, what other options do I have than letting you go and helping you get rid of my incapability to be the real me?

I want us to stick together and work at it, but how do I know you'll be able to bear it if you said you couldn't? How can you say that I'm not trying too hard? I'm afraid that if I'm selfish and beg you to stay and help me work at it, you'll look back to our months together as a total waste. Your happiness means a lot to me.

It's now 12:55 a.m. Are you sure you'll feel OK if I go with you to Texas? I love you and God knows how much you mean to me.

Deb

* * *

Deb,

Thanks for the note. I was hoping that you would have written. Today's been rough. In between tears, I managed to complete my test (I feel confident) and take care of a few errands (bike box, car light, etc.). I'm really hurting inside; you mean so much to me, and yet the idea of ending our relationship is there – big as day.

I don't know, maybe you aren't really wanting this to work out. Last night and this morning I felt that you were letting go too fast. If that's the case, it wasn't worth the fight. Or, maybe I never knew what exactly I wanted from you or the relationship because I had no idea that I could place demands on you and it. That's my right as a partner, and yet I don't even know how. How can you give me what I want if you don't know what it is that I want?

I am learning to stop focusing on other people and take care of myself. To find out what I want, to be selfish, for a change. It's scary. I'm scared! It's gonna take a while. (Hard to teach an old dog new tricks. Ha!) I don't know if I'm making any sense. If you want to let me go, then remember that I'll still be your best friend. You and I started that way, remember? That will never change. I could never let you drop out of my life totally. You're always in my heart. So, I don't have a quick solution for us. If you can't handle the uncertainty, I understand. Meanwhile, I'll be learning those "new tricks." I love you Deb.

Peter

Chapter 43

Spring 1988

*D*espite our commotion in November and December, Peter had decided I was worth the fight. He chose to remain by my side. Apparently, he could see through the ugliness that was my life and had faith in whatever good he saw in me. Years later, he would describe what he saw in me as emotional intelligence and compelling inner beauty.

Although Peter professed his love for me daily, I found myself being on guard, questioning his authenticity. When he asked me about my day, I couldn't help but wonder if he was really interested. His life seemed so much more exciting than mine. The more he talked about himself, the more I resented him. I thought I had adjusted to not having friends, but that wasn't so. While I encouraged him to develop friendships, his going out at night hit me the hardest.

I wanted so badly to graduate alongside Peter. I wasn't sure if we'd still be romantically involved, but the idea of being on campus without him, alone again, was terrifying. I met with my academic advisor to see if I could somehow graduate on time, and I was granted permission to take classes beyond the standard eighteen credits.

On the outside, I appeared to be doing very well. With my twenty-credit course load, I made it to the Dean's List for a second semester in a row. To my surprise, my basketball coaches named me the Most Valuable Player though I had only started in a few games. On the inside, however, I was still a mess. Halfway through the semester, I wrote to Peter: "What

I'm going through is scary. More than anything, I want to be helped. I'm a little afraid that you will get tired of me and my problems, and won't want anything to do with me." Some days, I found myself crying over the most trivial things. At times, I was able to make connections between whatever happened that day and my tears, but, there were days I simply couldn't.

May came, and once again, I had survived another year at Gallaudet. Although I hated the thought of leaving Peter, I accepted a ten-week summer internship in Columbus, Ohio, working with Deaf foster kids. I had declared psychology as my major, and I felt I needed some experience in the field. When Peter and I parted, I had a sense of calm – we'd be OK. We wrote letters to each other often, and with Columbus only a half-day's drive, Peter visited me several weekends.

After a few weeks, Peter wrote:

> People always say that when you meet the right person, you'll know. Well, I guess that I realize more and more every day that you are the right person for me. My life is complete with you. Therefore, I want you to be my wife! I hope I didn't scare you off. If so, I am sorry. I love you so much and don't ever want to be without you. Having you as my wife, friend, lover, companion is and will be the greatest thing ever to happen to me. I just don't want to wait longer than I need to.

Peter hadn't scared me off, but I had felt some pressure from our relationship. I realized I had needed some time to take care of myself first, just like he had. But at the same time, I was afraid I would lose him if I kept him waiting. I'd never forgiven myself for having the affair with *him*, and I knew that feelings can change. That scared me. But I had dreamed often of being Peter's wife, so I responded: "There are things I don't know about myself yet, and I need to take some time to learn them. I love you, and I believe you love me. I have to admit, I like the thought of being your wife. You are the only one I want to spend the rest of my life with. You are my best friend."

But when would I be ready? I wasn't sure. All I knew was that I had to take care of myself before I could consider marrying Peter.

Chapter 44

August 1988

Peter was about to kiss me when I turned my head slightly, just in time for his lips to land on my cheek.

"You don't want me to kiss you," Peter said – more of a statement than a question.

"I'm sorry," I said. What else could I say?

"Did I do something wrong?" He asked. By now, he must have noticed I'd been avoiding his kisses deliberately.

"It's not you," I told him. "At least I don't think so." I could tell how crushed Peter was. I felt so guilty. What was happening? Something was very wrong; I knew that much, but beyond that, I wasn't sure.

I had arrived home from my summer internship, and Peter spent the weekend visiting me and my family. Now, thanks to me, he had left, feeling hurt and confused. I wrote him a letter shortly after, assuring him of my love for him.

I also wrote, "I guess there is a lot that is going on inside me, and as of right now, I just need you as a friend. Don't get me wrong, you've been one. What I mean is that I find myself not wanting to do anything with you physically. I don't know why, but I just want to be held, that's all. Whatever I said must have hurt you. I beg you to understand that it is also hard on me." I ended the letter with a request that he help me find a good counselor as soon as I returned to DC for my final year at Gallaudet.

Once back at school, I had my intake appointment with a therapist in a private practice who knew ASL. When I learned how much the sessions would cost, I was hesitant. I was never good at spending money on myself, and the thought of paying sixty dollars for a fifty-minute session seemed outrageous. Come to think of it, the therapist would be charging me a dollar per minute! I was not happy, but knew I needed help. My dilemma: How was I going to pay $240 each month?

I had to find a part-time job fast. So, at 5:30 on weekday mornings, I would begin my days rolling out freshly made dough at a T.J. Cinnamons bakery in downtown DC. Through the window, people's faces slowly became visible as daylight arrived. They stood in a line, waiting eagerly for the shop to open, so that they could purchase a cinnamon roll or two on their way to work. After the morning rush, several dozen rolls later, I would leave to attend my morning classes.

I was determined to graduate alongside Peter. I completed twenty-one credits in the first semester, and I ended the spring semester having completed nineteen. I almost quit playing basketball because I wasn't sure I could do it all. But after speaking to my coach, Kitty, she helped me figure out a way to remain on the team. On the days I had to fulfill my class projects, she allowed me to arrive for practice late or to leave early.

Along with everything happening in my life, I was having a rough time with my therapy sessions. Because I had to pay every dollar out of my pocket, I was determined to make the most of my sessions. I showed up ready to tackle my issues, often bringing along notes. In between sessions, I would jot down all the feelings that had surfaced, the arguments between Peter and I, the irrational thoughts that filled my mind, and just about anything I thought might be relevant or worth sharing. I *forced* myself to talk, and I was attentive to what the therapist had to say.

And, I cried *a lot*. Often, my tears continued throughout the day and into the night. My tears would return, as fresh as ever, when Peter and I talked about what had taken place during my sessions. Where did all the tears come from? They fell like a spring rain, hard and without warning.

Chapter 45

August 1989

I slid down slowly, my back against the wall, onto the bare, cold concrete deck of the ship. I didn't pay much attention to anyone crossing my path; there were many traveling in and out of the bathroom. My period began earlier in the day and I was already feeling sick. The constant rocking motion and the dampness in the air made it worse.

We were on the ferry on our way to picturesque Nova Scotia for our honeymoon. Peter had taken care of all the honeymoon arrangements and expenses. As avid bicyclists, we had brought along our bicycles, ready for our weeklong adventure.

The euphoria from the wedding was fast fading from memory.

Our honeymoon, excitement and all, would begin the following day, but it was hard to visualize – I was so caught up in my own misery.

Life is like a ferry. Often it sails out of the harbor smoothly. As it travels further out to sea, however, it runs into the unexpected. Doldrums – water so still you get restless. Fierce storms – huge waves that take you under. Pirates – attacks that hold you prisoner for the time being. Our destination may seem like a hopeless dream, but if we keep our eyes and mind set on the land, we eventually get there.

Chapter 46

Fall 1988 – Senior year

*I*n my high school yearbook, I listed "Whatever" as my favorite saying.

If I expressed an idea and someone disagreed with what I said, I would respond with, "Whatever." I avoided conflict at any cost by placing others' opinions before my own. If I was asked what I wanted, I would respond, "Whatever you want is fine with me." Surely others had preferences, and I didn't want to be too demanding.

"Whatever" to this. "Whatever" to that. My opinions stayed with me, always. My thoughts remained my own, always. My feelings were kept hidden, always. I was easy to please, or so everyone thought.

Peter was frustrated, however. Making decisions was very difficult for me. For instance, when asked which restaurant I would like to eat at, I was adept at shifting the decision back onto him, and we would end up going where he wanted to go. I brought up the issue in therapy.

"Where is Deb? Who is Deb? What does Deb like?" my therapist challenged me.

"I don't know," I said. A tear rolled down my cheek.

As my fifty-minute session neared the end, he reached for a book on his coffee table. He held out for me to see. I looked at the title: *The Missing Piece Meets the Big O* by Shel Silverstein.

"Have you ever read this book?" He asked.

"No," I said. "I've heard of the author though. I think I read some of his poems when I was in middle school."

"Good. Take the book home. I want you to read. Bring it back next week, and we'll talk more." Our session was over; he always ended our hour precisely on time.

I walked out of his office, out of the building, onto the parking lot, and opened the door to my car. As soon as I flopped into the front seat, I opened the book to the first page.

"The missing piece sat alone…"

I flipped to the next page, "…waiting for someone to come along and take it somewhere."[1]

I finished reading the entire book, which only took me a few minutes. Then, I read it again. And, during the next several days, I read the book who knows how many times. I even went to the bookstore to buy a copy of my own.

It was so simple. And so true.

I realized that my life could not be "whatever." I mattered. My thoughts and opinions mattered. My preferences mattered. My life must be whole, I must be complete – independent emotionally – before I could expect to become interdependent relationally. Peter and I would grow only as I became my own person.

My life as the selfless daughter, the easy-going friend, the timid student, and the self-sacrificing person was really no life at all.

Therapy – and a simply powerful book – had begun to open my eyes to the life I wanted, life as it could be. And, as I later realized, life as God intended. A rich life. An emotion-filled life. A life to be shared fully, without pretense, secrets, or "whatevers."

I wanted this life. Yet there was still so much I needed to learn.

---

1 Shel Silverstein, The Missing Piece and the Big O (New York: Harper Collins, 1981).

Chapter 47

Fall 1988

id your mom ever follow through on her suicidal talk?" my therapist asked.

"While I grew up, no," I said. And, then I remembered: "She attempted suicide once."

"She did?"

"Yes. It happened when she was twenty-one."

"Tell me more."

"Mom was unhappy. She was having a hard time at home, so she moved out and lived with a Deaf couple. Her life continued to be miserable, so she decided to end it by swallowing a bottle full of pills. She blacked out. The couple found her on the floor, and they called in an ambulance. The next thing Mom knew, she was in the hospital, still alive. The pills she swallowed had been pumped out of her stomach."

"So, you were burdened with the fact that she had tried it, and when she threatened about going into the garage, you knew she was capable of attempting suicide?"

"I guess so," I said. I had not made the connection until now. "Yes, I was scared because I believed she could do it."

I was so young when Mom detailed her attempt. I don't remember the first time she told me the story. Perhaps it was when I asked about her wedding picture. This same Deaf couple who had found her blacked out was posed next to Mom and Dad. They had served as witnesses in the place of my grandparents who couldn't (or refused to) attend. I knew this couple. They visited us once in a while. In fact, they were the ones who gave us our first dog – a beautiful black cocker spaniel we named Blackie. Or perhaps, the first time she had told me of her attempt was when she'd threatened to go into the garage.

Regardless of when she first told me, the truth is that for most of my life, I knew about her suicide attempt. I just hadn't realized until now the impact it had had on me. Every time she threatened to go into the garage, I believed she would do it. After all, she tried it once; she could try it again.

Mom's typical response to any conflict was: "I wish I could die, then I would be at peace." Apparently, Mom had never learned to handle conflict or confrontation. In turn, she would make us feel guilty for her own anxiety over the conflict, manipulating us with words like, "I know you wouldn't care if I die."

I had unconsciously adopted her way of thinking and embraced her behavior. I would give people the silent treatment when I was upset with them. That was the only way I knew how to respond. When my friends fought, I became very uncomfortable. When my friends were hurt emotionally, they would work through the pain and move on with their lives. However, I would wish I could die.

But I learned. When emotions would overwhelm me during a therapy session, my therapist would ask: "What is the worst outcome possible in that scenario?" After several sessions, working through worst-case scenarios, I realized I could, in fact, live through it. I *would* live through it.

Both time and practice created greater distance between episodes. And after several years, I had finally been set free from my irrational thinking.

Chapter 48

Fall 1988

Why *he* was on campus that day, I don't recall. What I remembered was our conversation in the parking lot, behind the Peet Hall dormitory.

"You need to talk to someone," I pleaded. I was really concerned; he was still grieving. It had been over a year since I'd left him, and he was not doing very well.

"Like who?"

"I don't know," I said, feeling helpless. "Someone you can trust. One of your friends, perhaps?" I saw the value in sharing with someone – I had Peter. I also had just begun attending therapy. Seeing a counselor wasn't an option, he said.

"There has to be someone," I said, trying to think. After coming up with several names, I thought of someone – a friend of his who had moved to a different state.

"Maybe I could talk to her," he agreed.

"Or maybe even someone from the psychology department at MSD?" I suggested. I figured that their policy would require staff to keep information confidential. At the time, I didn't realize the complexity of our relationship; how the disclosure could land him in prison. During the two and half years we were together, I was mostly fearful about his wife finding out. I hadn't considered that I was a minor and that it was against the law for an adult to be involved with a seventeen-year-old.

When we departed, he promised he'd talk to someone. And he did – both the female friend I had suggested and a staff member from the psychology department. The next time

I saw him I asked if he'd talked to them, and he said he had. Talking to those two people had helped just a little. Then he told me he had written poems about his brokenness over the end of our relationship.

I must have asked to read them, because he sent me copies of them. One read:

Although we were
    Worlds apart
We fell in Love
    And stole each other's hearts

Friends forever
    Or so it seemed
Fell in Love
    Because of our dreams

Afraid to touch
    Across the hands of time
I was yours
    You were mine

Somehow our eyes
    Would always meet
Together
    The hugs were extra neat

Happy
    In the world we knew
Life was mean
    Oh so cruel

Being together
    You and I
I saw the feelings
    Watched you cry

Walks together
In a mountain park
Hand in hand – heart in heart
Heart and heart

Good times together
Is what we had
Made me happy
Made you sad

So much together
The time we spent
Came so fast
Then it went

Happy together
And what's more
Only you'll know
I say at four

Walks by the river
Initials in a tree
Love forever
As it was meant to be

We left our mark
For the world to see
It stands alone
A single tree

So much pleasure
Being with you then
Will it return
I wonder when

The way things are
    (guess they) were meant to be
Me alone
    While you are free

Alone for now
    For you have gone
Strong feelings
    Love lives on

I Love Yous
    Were always true
From the (young) girl I knew
    A Lady grew

There were twelve poems. They were each typewritten on 8 1/2 × 11 paper and were bound with a cover page entitled: "What Can I Say!!!"

He had said it all. What could I have said? I have no recollection of my reaction to reading them, but I know I experienced several emotions through the years, all of which had come and gone except for one – guilt. And it stayed with me for a very long time.

Chapter 49

May 1989

The day I thought would never come had finally arrived. I walked across the stage in my graduation gown to receive my diploma, graduating *cum laude*. But also, on my left ring finger was an engagement ring – our wedding was two and a half months away.

I had suspected Peter would propose on Christmas Day, but it was Thanksgiving morning when he slid the ring onto my finger. I wasn't ready but I was making progress in therapy. I wanted an autumn wedding, but Peter didn't want to wait. So we settled for August.

By the time I graduated, I had been in therapy for almost a year. With the wedding approaching, I was experiencing wedding jitters. As much as I was looking forward to being Peter's wife, I knew we had issues that we needed to address. So I invited Peter to join me for a few therapy sessions.

My chief concern was the nature of our relationship – I was Deaf; he was hearing. All my life, Mom had drilled into me to never marry a hearing man. Her message was direct: hearing men could not be trusted. As always, Mom had stories to tell: The phone would ring. The hearing husband would pick up the phone. The Deaf wife would ask who called. He would inform her that it was his mom. He would chat and laugh for a length of time, in front of her. A few days later, another call. This time, it would be his sister. And his wife would be clueless that on the other end of the phone was actually his mistress. Another story: The couple would attend a gathering with mostly hearing people. Everyone would talk nonstop. The wife would ask what the conversation was about. He would say that it was nothing important and that he would explain later. Then, when he did, he would merely summarize the entire conversation in a sentence or two. She would feel completely isolated and left out.

Mom was not the only one who was concerned. Bridgetta also cautioned me. She meant well, and I must admit that I had given the same advice to others, but my faith in Peter and our relationship surpassed my fears. Nevertheless, there were Deaf/hearing issues that I wanted to address. I later learned that some of these were actually related to our roles as man and woman or our pasts. For example:

Music. Every time Peter walked into the house or got into the car, he would automatically turn on music. I didn't understand the value of music. As ridiculous as it may have seemed, I was jealous. I felt I had to compete with the radio to get his attention. When I wanted to talk to him or needed his attention, he was easily distracted.

Outings. When we went out for dinner, Peter would order food for both of us. Since I'd assumed the caregiver/parental role growing up, I interpreted Peter's behavior as paternalistic that I wasn't "able." I would ignore him when he asked my preference and proceed to tell the waitress myself.

Intelligence. When Peter used big words, on papers or in communicating with others, it reinforced my feeling of inferiority. I was worried that I wouldn't be good enough for Peter, and he would one day regret marrying me. Also, Peter always seemed to have access to information, and I was concerned that he would one day tire of filling me in.

Finally, I wasn't the only one with baggage. Peter had also come from a dysfunctional family. He was the youngest of four, and his mother had married three times. The last time Peter had seen his biological father was when he was seven. Peter's second stepfather adopted him and his three siblings. His new "dad," also a divorcee, had served in the Vietnam and Korean wars. He was not able to express feelings other than anger. By the time Peter reached middle-school, he realized that his mom was an alcoholic, and he had to deal with her constant lying.

We had so many issues to work on. Our few sessions had turned into one year of work together. In the meantime, our wedding plans were underway.

Chapter 50

July 1989

very day, I waited eagerly to see who had responded; at least one RSVP card would land in our mailbox. I laughed when I read the card from Aunt Marlene. She put down five for the number of people attending the wedding. Below, she scribbled: "P.S. Hope you don't mind, Rachel is bringing her *friend* (BOY). Don't say anything to Bill!!"

Grandma, who had lived next door all my life, even bothered to mail me the card. I was surprised when I saw the number she had put down – 100. I never knew she had a sense of humor. How much deeper our relationship, my life, would have been if we were able to communicate without paper and pencil.

The topic of our conversation at the table during supper was always whose card would arrive the next day. Many relatives were able to witness our wedding – several aunts and uncles from Mom's side of the family, and all great-aunts and great-uncles from Dad's side, not to mention cousins. Deaf people from Mom and Dad's circle of friends with whom I had grown up wouldn't miss the wedding – they were like a family. MSD coaches, teachers, and classmates were also invited. To cover up my lack of friends at Gallaudet, I had invited my basketball teammates.

Most of the regrets came from Peter's family and friends. Maryland was so far away from Texas; to travel for the wedding would have been too costly. Some of those unable to attend had mailed us gifts.

Among the gifts we received, one stood out: a handmade

picture from Peter's church family. A 16 × 20 frame with blue matting was cut in the shape of a house. Inside the house, a calligrapher had skillfully adorned everyone's written comments using different fonts and styles. There was a small cross at the top.

In one corner, along the edge of the house, was a letter from Rev. Robert Brown, Peter's pastor: "Pete and Debbie, it was a pleasant surprise and a happy one to read about your upcoming marriage. Sorry it is so distant from us. We would be there otherwise. Marriage is such a rich and satisfying experience to those who are willing to sacrifice selfish ideas and patterns of action and work together, both to please each other and also, above all else, to please God in Christ."

A member had advised: "Remember always to set aside time for each other, to share your feelings and thoughts both good and bad, to laugh and enjoy life along the way. Always keep the Lord first, and you'll have a long and love-filled life."

One had listed ten rules for a happy marriage:

1. Never both be angry at once.

2. Never yell at each other unless the house is on fire.

3. If you must criticize, do it lovingly.

4. Never bring up a mistake of the past.

5. Neglect the whole world but not each other.

6. Never let the day end without one compliment to each other.

7. Never meet without an affectionate greeting.

8. Never go to bed mad.

9. When you've made a mistake, talk it out and ask for forgiveness.

10. It always takes two to make an argument. The one doing the most of the talking is usually wrong.

One had written a verse from the Bible: "For this reason a man shall leave his father and his mother, and be united to his wife; and they shall become one flesh." (Gen. 2:24).

Still another had written: "A husband and wife must always be willing to compromise. Though your life together will have joy, sorrow, and hardships, always take them to God in prayer. Also, read the Holy Bible regularly. The Bible has the answers for work, marriage, raising a family, and all the other things we experience in life. Again, congratulations and may the grace and peace of our Lord Jesus Christ be with you and your wife to be, for ever more."

The theme was centered on God and Jesus Christ. Keeping the Lord first. Reading the Holy Bible. The Bible having the answers for marriage. And pleasing the Lord.

The fact that the church family had taken the time and effort to create such a masterpiece touched me. The significance of the words passed on to us was *nice,* but at the time, it meant nothing more. I hadn't realized the significance God played in marriages – that marriage was His idea, intended to glorify Him. Had I known, Peter and I might have been saved a lot of frustration and struggle early in our life together.

Other than those instructions, no one had told me how marriage takes work – a lot of hard work. I had learned about my role as a wife from Mom, but she wasn't the one to emulate. Grandma could have had been a role model, but Grandpa had died when I was three. I'd assumed Grandmother and Grandfather had a solid marriage; after all, they had been married for sixty-one years. But I really didn't know them.

At last, our big day had arrived; Grandma's pastor had

proclaimed us husband and wife, one flesh in God's sight. I stepped out of the church with a new name – Mrs. Myers.

And with no formal instructions or guidance on how to be a wife, I would be pretty much on my own for the first ten years of marriage.

Chapter 51

October 1989

*P*eter and I walked into the apartment that would be our new home for the next ten months. We had been married two months when I was hired at MSD as a dormitory counselor working with middle school girls. On each floor of the dormitory were two apartments, one on each end of the wing, for counselors wishing to rent. In addition to a tiny bathroom, the apartment consisted of only two bare rooms of cinderblock painted a dull yellow color.

The rent was cheap compared to our first apartment – a little over a hundred dollars a month. Since it was connected to the dormitory building, our electricity and water were included. Living on campus would enable us to save a lot of money for our two upcoming trips – one to California, for Peter's brother's wedding, and the other our bicycle trip across America.

The apartment also came with doubts. How would we cook our meals? There was no kitchen – not even a stove or refrigerator. And we weren't sure where we could find used appliances at good price. Not only that, there was no kitchen sink for us to wash our dirty dishes in – we would have to use the bathroom tub.

Several days after we moved in, I bumped into *him* on campus. I told him about our challenging living arrangement, and he said he had a used refrigerator that had been sitting in *his* garage waiting to find a home. He would sell it to us for $100. Perfect.

So Peter and I made a trip to his house.

When we walked into his kitchen, memories suddenly flooded my mind; though I tried, I couldn't stop myself reliving them.

How I wished that I hadn't made the trip to his house before I left for Texas. If only I had known then the depth of God's love for me. If only I had known that God had bigger plans for me. If only I had known that I would meet Peter. If only I had waited until my wedding night. "If only's" were worthless now. I had naively taken matters into my own hands, believing there was no hope in my future. And, in the end, I had given all of myself to him.

Peter took my hand, bringing me back to the present as we were led into *his* garage to see the refrigerator. We hauled it onto the back of a pick-up truck we had borrowed. Back on the road, Peter turned to me and asked: "Are you okay?"

"I think so," I said. But I really wasn't. Seeing the house, replaying the lovemaking scene, and knowing he remained married had stirred feelings in me. Later, that week, I penned in my journal: "How my mood had changed when I was at his place to pick up the refrigerator. I wondered if he had really loved me? If he did, why didn't he leave his wife? Did he use me? My gosh, I was only seventeen. I was a kid! He was so much an adult, and yet, he was with me. I was young and so naïve. I trusted him. I needed him. He was a father figure I looked up to, and I got myself mixed up with the need for affection and attention. Did he go with other ladies? Was I the only – the only lady? I thought my feelings were resolved. We're friends. Working on the same campus is something I thought I could deal with. But, no, feelings are still there."

As much as I had wanted to leave my past behind me, it followed me. After all, it was a part of me. It had shaped me. It had changed me.

Chapter 52

May 1990

I thought I'd never step foot on the campus again – ever. Unfortunately, whenever mentioned, Gallaudet triggered unpleasant thoughts and feelings in me. The fact that everyone else lionized the school and their experience there made it even more difficult.

The Deaf community is so small, there is always a connection somewhere, somehow. So for many years afterward, I had to endure all the questions Deaf people ask:

"You graduated from Gallaudet? What year?"

"1989."

"1989? I was a member of Class of 1987. I should know you." After trying to recognize me without much success, this person would then ask: "Who were your circle of friends?"

How I hated this question. As always, I was adept at deflecting. I had my well-rehearsed answer that worked every time.

"You know Tiffany? Bridgetta? David?" I would say, adding several other well-known classmates of mine from high school.

"Yes."

"We grew up together."

"Ah. Maryland School. Good group of people." As soon as that connection was made, our conversation would proceed to other subjects; thankfully, the topic of Gallaudet would pass.

But, in fact, I did return to Gallaudet a year later.

As my therapy progressed, I couldn't help thinking of all the people who could benefit from the same kind of care I received. I wanted to help others lead healthy, well-adjusted, and productive lives. When I learned that Gallaudet offered a master's degree in mental health counseling, with Peter's and my therapist's encouragement, I applied.

My therapist wrote one of my letters of recommendation:

Deb is a woman of quiet power. Initially, she comes across as quiet and reserved but as one gets to know her, one sees the magnitude of her inner strength. She is extremely bright and insightful and works hard to achieve her goals. Interpersonally, she can be wonderfully engaging, direct, and powerful. Her self-insight and her keen sense of the needs of others allow her to connect with people at a deeper level of understanding. In such interactions, Deb manages to be both caring and direct. She is not afraid to speak out about her point of view and yet she maintains openness to the point of view of others.

Most importantly, she is highly motivated to learn about herself and to grow both personally and professionally. During the time I have worked with her, I have witnessed enormous personal growth as she has struggled with her inner issues and conflicts. She demonstrates the type of commitment to her therapy and personal growth that is so important for both graduate students and professionals in the field of mental health.

My basketball coach recommended me as well:

I have known Debbie for the past five years as her teacher, coach, and friend. Debbie is an honest, trustworthy, conscientious, responsible, and dependable person. She has the ability to adjust quickly to new situations and needs little or no direction or supervision. She is a thinking individual who can and does contribute ideas.

During her career as an undergraduate student at Gallaudet University, Debbie was faced with a variety of academic, social, and personal challenges which she faced head-on with composure and introspection. Throughout this time Debbie demonstrated a level of maturity indicative of a person many years older. Debbie's leadership style and intuitive thinking set her apart from the rest.

I knew I was honest and trustworthy. I knew I was quiet and reserved. I knew I could be direct if given the opportunity to voice my thoughts and feelings. I knew I was mature beyond my age. But, a woman of quiet power? Extremely bright? A leadership style that set me apart from the rest?

For the next several days, I couldn't stop thinking about what my therapist and coach had written. To finally believe in myself was a process that had taken so many years. But I was finally beginning to see the woman that God had created me to be. Through the help of my therapist and Peter's reassuring love, God was laying the foundation for a transformed life.

Chapter 53

March 1991

I sighed as I read the letter from the vice principal at Williamsport High School asking if we could meet. My brother, David, was failing his senior year.

"He must graduate," I told Peter. "I won't let him fail."

"I know, but he must have the desire to graduate," Peter said.

"Right. But if he has the desire, who will help him?" I was frustrated. I wanted to help and it was hard being an hour and half away. I was twenty-three, into my first year of graduate school. Being the oldest, all of this fell on my shoulders.

And, now a letter from Connie had just arrived in the mail. I pondered our upbringing:

Debbie. Connie.
Deaf. Hearing.
Oldest. Middle child.
ASL. English.
Lived in the dorm. Lived at home.
No church. Grew up in church.

Despite our differences, we were affected just the same.

I remembered how Connie had slipped a note to me when she was fifteen. I was seventeen:

Hey Sis, I need to talk to someone, and I guess it is going to be you. I have a problem. I can't get along with Mom and Dad anymore . . . All my life I guess I never really felt like I was a part of the family. Do you know in my entire life I have only been hugged about five times, and none of them by our parents? Do you know how jealous I am of Debbie [her best friend] because almost every day her parents tell her they love her? I have never been told that by them . . . Lately, I read about teenage suicides. Don't get worried 'cause I'm not going to kill myself; I think it's dumb, but I just can't stop thinking about this . . .

Then, when she was twenty, Connie had written me a letter. I had just gotten married:

Well, hello stranger! I just got your letter today, which was something I really needed . . . Out of all my semesters here, I don't think I have ever felt so alone than this one. No one is willing to be there except for themselves and that is so hard for me to accept or see . . . sometimes I just wish I could start over because I feel like I am just surrounded by walls and no way out . . . A lot of times it seems like you are the only one in the whole family that cares about me at all . . . I'm doing a project in one of my classes that requires me to be more positive toward myself. I am learning how to accept compliments but I don't think it is working too well. For a while I was doing great but then it just seemed like everything just died . . .

A year later, Connie had written again. I had just started my graduate studies at Gallaudet.

I am sorry I haven't written but I really needed time to just sit and think about everything that has happened . . . When I was growing up, you weren't around to see

how hard David and I had it. At least you could leave
and go back to school. We had to stay and live through
it . . . It always seemed as if I were there to do things
for everyone else. What I did didn't matter at all!
When I noticed how you and David got attention with
injuries, I took a brick and smashed it on my ankles
for weeks, hoping it would break or something so that
someone would notice me! I have never been able to
express what I feel without someone saying, "Oh come
on." Or better yet, they just ignore me.

When I got into high school and met Charlie, I thought
he was a godsend. He got me so involved in school
activities that I was away constantly. He treated me like
dirt a lot, but I was willing to take his abuse over the
pain I always felt at home. I wanted to leave Charlie a
long time ago, but no one would have ever known that.
My reasoning was quite simple, he was the one escape
from everything that I had . . . Finally, I got the courage
to do it and stopped seeing him. Even though I knew I
would be totally alone except for God . . .

. . . The one thing I don't understand is how you can
say you don't like what I have become. I love what I
am now and am very happy . . . The one major factor
that has influenced my change is that I am actually
thinking of myself for a change . . . I am growing to
love myself and now the one person I thought would
be happy for me doesn't like it. Well, I am sorry, but
I like the person I am and I have adapted myself for
everyone all of my life so this is the person I want
to be. There are so many things that you don't know
about me and I know I could never tell you 'cause you

just wouldn't understand my reasoning at all. No one ever will!

Several months later, another letter came:

Hello Sis! My classes are going pretty good . . . David seems to be doing okay. He really wants to go to the prom but feels that he is too stupid for a girl to go out with. His self-esteem is really low when it comes to certain things. I tried to help him as much as I could but I'm not really the one to talk either . . . I did want to thank you for talking to me last week on the phone. I have wanted to talk about this for a while and I guessed that you would be the best person. Working it out myself really hasn't helped that much. Whenever it is okay with you I would really like to talk to you. Maybe you can straighten me out. Ha!

Debbie. Connie. David.
Girl. Girl. Boy.
Oldest. Middle. Last.
ASL. English. English.
Sports. Drama. Sports.

Despite our differences, we had the same need – to be loved. There was no question we were affected by our upbringing, but that didn't necessarily mean that Mom and Dad didn't love us. I had written in my journal: "After going through therapy, even though I talked negatively about my parents' method of raising me, I love them more. I, now, can accept the past and draw the line between my love and respect for them and the 'hatred' I felt for being screwed up."

I made a choice – to forgive them and to move on with my life.

Chapter 54

1989 – 1997

The first eight years of our marriage were like a roller coaster. What a ride it had been! One night several months after Peter and I had been married I walked around inside the mall and wondered about our life together. We'd had our share of good days, but we'd had our bad days as well. In fact, we had quarreled a lot. Had I made a terrible mistake? With *him,* I'd never fought.

But then, with *him,* I had no expectations in our relationship. His life had been well grounded. He had a career. He was married. He was a father. My schedule had always revolved around his. We would get together at 4:00 p.m. on Fridays after he left work. And we would depart in time for him to be home with his family for supper. His life dictated our life.

With Peter, however, I found myself wanting a say. I placed high expectations on him and on us. And when my expectations were not met, our discussions often escalated into arguments.

Like Dad, Peter had a strong work ethic. But unlike Dad, who would clock in and out of work at the same time every day, Peter would either work late or bring his work home. I found myself preparing homemade meals only to have them turn cold when Peter arrived home late. When Peter was home, I wanted his full attention, and when he didn't give it, I became upset.

As much as I believed Peter wouldn't do such a thing, there were a few times early in our marriage when I had wondered about Peter coming home late *again.* If *he* was capable of cheating on his wife, could Peter?

And speaking of infidelity, I was horrified when I thought

of *him* while Peter and I made love. Not that I wanted him. I just couldn't seem to escape my past. It continued to haunt me. After several weeks – perhaps, it had been months – the thoughts eventually went away. The first couple of years were a confusing time for me. I didn't understand why I wasn't responding to Peter's touches as I did with him. Neither of us had recognized the impact my affair had on me. Peter and I terminated our therapy without resolving our issues surrounding sex. Although we had talked about it a little from time to time, bringing up the issue in therapy had been awkward and uncomfortable. I was not as affectionate as Peter would have liked. It was not my nature, and I understood I had to work harder at expressing myself. Our one year of work together was beneficial, yet sex was still the elephant in the room.

How I had wished that sex was not such a big deal; that we could have lived without it. It was giving us so much trouble. At the time, I lacked an understanding of how God created and designed men. I had always thought that for men, sex was simply for pleasure. No one had told me that sex was more than just a way of meeting his physical needs. As I later learned, sex is actually tied to men's emotional needs, and when their sexual needs are met, they feel loved and secure. Sex is also tied to a man's self-confidence. Withholding sex from a man would be the equivalent of his refusal to listen to a woman when she needed to talk.

The ride continued – the ups, exhilarating; the downs, terrifying.

One day, I gave Peter a card with this message printed on the inside: WE USED TO HAVE SO MUCH FUN TOGETHER. I DON'T KNOW WHAT WENT WRONG, BUT I REALLY MISS THE WAY WE USED TO BE. Below I had scribbled: "Peter, we need to decide whether or not to work on our marriage. I can't just go on like we are living now. I need to know if there's hope."

Was there hope?

Chapter 55

Early 1990s

I looked at the clock and let out a sigh. It was only 10:23 p.m. and I was tired. I really wanted to sleep, but it was still too early.

I walked into the kitchen and thought about putting away the dishes. No, that wouldn't be a good idea. That'd make too much noise. The last thing I wanted was to wake Peter; he had gone to bed around 10:10 p.m. I suppose I could read, but I wasn't in the mood. I went downstairs to the laundry room to sort our dirty clothes into three piles: white, color, and delicate. I would wash them tomorrow.

I wanted to sleep!

I went back upstairs and remembered that I hadn't paid the phone bill. *Might as well,* I thought. So, I sat down and wrote a check.

After thirty minutes Peter should have been asleep, or so I'd hoped. I went to bathroom for the last time, reminding myself not to flush. Then I tiptoed across the room and carefully slid into the left side of the bed without the slightest movement.

But as soon as I pulled the blanket to my chin, I felt Peter stirring. *Oh, no!* He rolled over on his side, his hand reaching over and landing on my stomach. I held my breath, praying silently: *Please, don't.* He then inched forward, pressing his body slightly against my back. *That was it.*

I immediately rolled over and got out of the bed. The lamp on his nightstand flicked on. I squinted, a bit exaggeratedly, adjusting to the sudden brightness.

"What's the matter?" I asked, acting naively. "I didn't mean to wake you."

Peter sat upright on the bed and responded angrily: "You know very well what the matter is. I'm tired of being rejected!"

"What are you talking about?" I maintained my innocence.

By now, Peter had gotten out of the bed. "I'm your husband. Yet, I can't even touch you." Peter looked at me. "Every time I try, you push me away. What did I do to deserve this?"

"Not true," I defended myself. "When you came home from work today, we hugged. Doesn't that count?"

"You know what I mean."

Now, it was my turn to get angry. "Sex-sex-sex! That's all you think about. You want sex? Fine. Go find someone! I don't care. I'm sure there are women who would love to have sex with you. Just go and leave me alone."

Peter looked at me, stunned. Then, he collapsed to his knees. And with his head in his hands, he sobbed. I'd never seen him like that before.

I felt a twinge of guilt but suppressed it. After all, he had deserved it. I was just tired of it all – avoiding him, walking on eggshells, the anxiety every night. Men seemed to have a one-track mind. And Peter was no better.

It was the same with *him*. Our hour together always started physically. Actually, we spent the majority of our time doing *that* rather than talking. And when we talked, it was he who did most of it. I had resented him for it.

Men are all alike. Even Mom thought the same way. She would tell me how tired she was in the morning, and when I asked her why, she would say: "Allen (she never referred him as 'Dad' when talking to me) wanted … you know men. He has passions and I can't say no. So, I gave in."

After several minutes, Peter looked up, sorrow clearly painted across his face. "Tell me you didn't mean that."

I thought about comforting him by telling him I didn't. But since I had spoken, I was determined not to take back my words. Instead, I said: "I can't satisfy you. So, what am I supposed to do? You are obviously not happy. Just go find someone who can."

"How could you?" Peter looked at me in disbelief. "You are my wife. You mean the world to me. If I have to choose, I would rather live without sex than not having you by my side."

"If sex isn't that important, then why are we having this discussion?" I challenged him.

"It's complicated," Peter stammered. "It's not so much the sex itself, though I do love that with you. Making love to you makes me feel *connected* to you," he explained.

Men and sex. That was something I didn't understand. But, I wasn't the only one. Peter didn't understand *my* needs either.

Chapter 56

Fall 1998

*H*ow I dreaded Sunday school class.

We had begun attending church when I was pregnant with our oldest daughter. Both of us agreed that it was important to raise our children in the church, yet despite our regular attendance for four years, I still didn't understand much. Who were those people the pastor kept referring to: Solomon, Paul, Isaiah, John? I had no idea.

Our church wasn't large; we met in the cafeteria of a middle school. Our worship service was interpreted. During the adult Sunday school hour, I managed to keep myself busy most of the time by tending to my children – breastfeeding, burping, and changing diapers. When they started walking, I would walk with them back and forth in the back of the room. When they became toddlers, I would sit on the floor and keep them occupied with books and toys.

But when our children were five, three, and one, we changed churches – to a much larger one. It had Sunday school classes for all ages – infants through adults. My youngest's feeding schedule did not coincide with the Sunday school hour, so with nothing to keep my hands full, I had no more excuses to avoid participating.

The teacher would ask the class a question, presumably something basic we all should know, and I would quickly look down at my Bible, pretending to read. In the meantime, out of the corner of my eye, I would watch for someone to answer. If the teacher asked a question I could answer, I was quick to raise my hand. I wasn't quite like a kindergartener who would boldly say: "Me! Me! I know the answer!" Rather, I would answer the question then breathe a sigh of relief, knowing that I could relax for the next few rounds of questions.

The pattern was exhausting. I was embarrassed that I wasn't familiar with the stories, stressed over not knowing the answers, anxious over the possibility of being asked a question, worried over what others would think if I gave an incorrect answer, and constantly reminded that I knew nothing. It all made me feel stupid.

So, when a Sunday school teacher for the Deaf elementary class needed a break for several months, I was quick to volunteer. "I'll be happy to teach." Not because I had a heart for teaching. Not because I had the desire to see the children grow in their knowledge of the Bible. Not because I wanted to reach out to them. I was thinking only of myself – an easy way out of my Sunday school class. I figured that the children wouldn't know more than I did.

God knew just what I needed. For the time being, I was comfortable. I was learning along with the little children in a nonthreatening setting. What I learned, I would share with my own children at home. And when I had questions during my preparation time, I had Peter to help me.

But like the Bible says, an infant cannot remain on milk forever (c.f., 1 Cor. 3:2). God knew I had to learn the basics before I could move on to the deeper material. I didn't know at the time that I would have to begin eating solid food eventually.

Chapter 57

1993 – 1998

*M*y children adored my mom and dad. They would wait anxiously by the window in our living room for their arrival. The minute Mom and Dad's car pulled into our driveway, they'd rush down the stairs, open the front door, and run into their arms.

Yes, they *hugged*.

Connie and I had started hugging them too. It had felt unnatural and awkward in the beginning, but as time progressed, it got easier. In fact, Mom and Dad had grown accustomed to being hugged and even expected it when we saw each other. Then, when the kids came along, hugging became natural for everyone.

Our kids would actually *kiss* Mom and Dad on the mouth. Not me, though. The only time Dad kissed me was on my wedding day, and that was something I was fine with. As a young girl, I may have envied my friends when their daddies kissed them, but as I grew, I couldn't imagine it otherwise.

Mom and Dad played a significant role in our children's lives. Mom was our children's caregiver when I worked. Mom was a fun grandmother; on the floor, interacting with our children all day long.

After working as a mental health therapist for several years, I returned to MSD, working part-time as a family educator. I traveled all over the state of Maryland visiting families with identified deaf children, birth through age five. Week after week, we taught parents ASL, modeled how to interact with their deaf child, and answered any questions they may have had about deafness and Deaf culture. We were delighted to see progress made by families who were eager to learn. Unfortunately, some parents had downplayed the significance of communicating with their child in ASL. As a result, their deaf children would begin school significantly behind their peers – both academically and socially.

Unlike me, Mom and Dad spent the first five years of their lives without any real communication. Such services provided by MSD didn't exist back then. Did Mom and Dad know the alphabet before entering school? Were they able to rote count to ten? Were they able to express their basic needs?

Mom's deafness wasn't discovered until she was two. Being the baby in a large family, I could only imagine her being passed between siblings to be fed, bathed, and clothed. Mom and Grandmother communicated with each other using homemade gestures or paper and pencil. Whenever we'd visit, we would sit in silence.

Grandma, however, knew basic survival signs – enough to get simple messages across. When Dad became Deaf at age three due to whooping cough, he was taken to different doctors in hopes his deafness could be cured. After unsuccessful attempts, Dad was enrolled in a residential school.

It's difficult to imagine growing up in a home without full access to communication, although I had a glimpse of what it was like when visiting relatives. Sadly, Mom and Dad's window to learning during the crucial years had been closed. So much was missed. How much did their limited communication at home contribute to how they raised me? There are no definite answers; I can only speculate.

Mom and Dad never witnessed loving or encouraging words exchanged between their parents. When Mom cried, she never received comforting words. When grandparents argued (if they did) or faced crises, Dad was not able to learn how they resolved conflicts. When rules and expectations were articulated, Mom probably learned them through trial and error. And what happened when Mom and Dad misbehaved? Who did they turn to when they needed someone to listen after a bad day?

Yet despite their difficult beginnings, they had learned through life and grown as parents and grandparents. Our children experienced the best of both worlds – they understood where their grandparents had come from, accepted their shortcomings, respected them as individuals, and loved them wholeheartedly.

Chapter 58

November 1998

We entered the room to discover a huge wooden cross laid in the center of the floor. Folding chairs encircled the cross; underneath each seat was a piece of paper and pencil. Forty-four ladies and I took our seats.

I had reluctantly left home two days earlier for the women's retreat. I didn't want to leave behind my children, but since this was the third time someone had offered to sponsor me, Peter encouraged me to accept the invitation. He reassured me that the kids would be fine, so I packed my belongings for the three-night retreat – ambivalent and nervous.

We received our instructions regarding what to do with the paper and pencil. The room turned silent as we pondered the things we wanted to nail to the cross – a metaphor for letting go of the burdens that interfered with and even worked against the life God had in store for us.

I knew immediately what I needed to let go of: *him*.

It had been eleven years since I found the strength to leave him.

I had long since forgiven him for the pain he caused me. The anger that I had experienced when I returned to Gallaudet for my junior year was short-lived. Later, when I learned that he was still having a hard time getting over me, my anger became pity, then guilt.

Guilt for causing him so much grief.

Guilt over our affair. I felt responsible for the whole thing.

I'd been carrying guilt for the past eleven years. It had haunted me every time I was reminded of him.

I sat and pondered all of this. I hadn't yet mustered the courage to write down his name. One by one, ladies rose from their seats and took their turns swinging the hammer. It was emotional for many, evidenced by the tears and sorrow on their faces. Some would complete the activity without expressing much at all. Others would break down, sobbing. Some would share what they had written; others couldn't.

Was it possible that God could forgive me for what I had done? For reasons I did not understand, it was easier for me to forgive *him* than to forgive myself. I wanted to believe I could be forgiven. I knew I needed to be forgiven.

At last, I wrote his name, praying silently, begging God for His forgiveness. I folded the paper in half and then into quarters before standing. I picked up a thick nail, walked toward the cross, knelt beside it, placed the folded paper onto the wood, and pounded the nail through the center.

I did not say a single word. There was no need. This was between the Lord and me. Though my hand was shaking, I managed to hit the nail harder the second time. I pounded repeatedly until the nail drove deeply into the wood. All of it – the affair, the guilt – was now Christ's.

I had made a terrible mistake. Whether it was my fault or not, it couldn't be undone. Yet it could be forgiven.

It was forgiven.

I was forgiven.

Chapter 59

December 1998

My heart raced as I prayed silently that Peter would do a good job. I knew practically everyone in the congregation, and I was worried about what they would think.

In front of me, in the pulpit, Peter stood. A few weeks earlier, he had talked to someone about the church's vacant pastoral position. The church we were attending had been without a permanent pastor for ten years and was seeking one for its Deaf congregation. That's why Peter was standing in the pulpit – he was invited as a guest speaker to preach the sermon.

Just before my attending the women's retreat, Peter had dropped the bomb. He informed me that he had been thinking about changing his career – going into the ministry and possibly becoming a pastor. "It is something that has been nudging me for some time," he said.

"You? A pastor? Are you kidding?" I responded, without thinking.

"I'm serious."

"I am sorry," I said. "But I just can't imagine you being a pastor." It was the truth. Peter as a pastor? No way. Not that he wasn't a good person. He was. Not that he wasn't compassionate. He was. Not that he couldn't relate to people easily. He could. Not that that he didn't know ASL well enough. He signed fluently. I couldn't figure out exactly what it was. All I knew was that I just could not imagine him being a pastor.

At the women's retreat, I had listened to Julie, one of the presenters, share her testimony. Since she was a little girl, all she'd ever wanted to be was a pastor's wife. Unbelievable. Why would anyone long to be a pastor's wife?

Then, it hit me. It wasn't that I couldn't imagine Peter being a pastor. I couldn't, I just couldn't, imagine myself being a pastor's wife. How could I possibly hold such a title if I knew so little about the Bible? What's more, I'd always been an introvert, reserved and quiet. How would that work at church socials?

By the end of Peter's sermon, I was awed. He delivered it with clarity. And, for the first time, I clearly understood God's message. That night, after our bedtime routine – giving our kids baths, serving their snack, reading aloud, and tucking them in – I sat down with Peter on the sofa.

"You were so good," I confessed.

"You really think so?" Peter asked, looking relieved.

I recognized what I needed to do. I had to put aside my fears and my pride. Deaf people deserved to have a pastor. How would I fill such a role as a pastor's wife? I wasn't sure.

"If you feel that's your calling, I'll give you my full support," I said.

God's ways are mysterious. In this move for our family, God had answered one of my prayers – the one I had prayed since my conversation with Bridgetta when I was thirteen. I had wanted to learn more about God and His Word, but every time I'd opened the Bible, I felt overwhelmed. So, I quit trying. But God didn't give up on me.

In fact, I would learn more than I'd imagined I could learn. And although my role as a pastor's wife would be challenging, even unpleasant at times, I recognized years later that He had allowed the experiences, the relationships, the loneliness, and the mistakes I'd made to prepare me for my new role at Peter's side.

Chapter 60

August 1999

With my hands in the air, I squealed as our car sped down the twisted roller coaster track at Hershey Park. It was Tuesday, the least crowded day of the week. There were no long lines, so we hopped from one ride to another all day long.

Walking hand in hand toward the next ride, I looked at Peter and admitted, "I wish we could have an extra day or two together."

It was our tenth anniversary getaway. Peter had wanted to escape for a week, but I didn't want to be away from our children that long. We negotiated, and I agreed reluctantly to a four-day trip. We had brought along our bicycles, wanting to explore back roads in New York. Unfortunately, on our way to a bed and breakfast, our bicycle rack broke, sending our bicycles somersaulting through the air before landing on the shoulder. Thankfully, no car was behind us, but our bicycles were beyond repair.

So instead, we spent the next two days strolling along small town main streets and exploring charming shops. We dined at various restaurants. And on our way home, we made an unplanned stop at Hershey Park for our last day together.

It was during this trip that I found myself falling in love with Peter all over again. I was pleasantly surprised at my responses to Peter's sexual advances – I had welcomed them and enjoyed our loving moments together. I even shed joyous tears during our lovemaking – we were going to be okay!

This breakthrough didn't happen overnight though. After

eight years of marriage, I had turned to the Lord and begged Him for his mercy. Each time Peter and I made love, I began praying silently before and during our lovemaking: "Lord, help me get through this. Help me relax. Help me." I couldn't seem to allow myself to enjoy the sexual experience. Years of misuse of sex by others too early in my life, a lack of appreciation and understanding for sex within marriage, and the guilt of the affair all had culminated in making this part of our lives miserable, but we felt like we were turning a corner.

Our trip also awakened us to the fact that we needed time together (alone) on a regular basis. I had never seen Mom and Dad go out on dates, and didn't see the need. But I learned. With young children, work schedules, and tight budgets, it was difficult to follow through. But we managed to be creative. When the kids were young, we'd excuse them from table after supper while we remained for thirty minutes to catch up with each other. Our kids quickly learned not to disturb our conversation. On Wednesdays, we'd send our kids to bed thirty minutes early so that we could have a late candlelight dinner. As the kids grew older, Peter and I spent evenings together after their bedtime – eating our dessert and talking. During their teen years, our older kids gladly babysat our youngest two so that we could go out for dinner or a walk.

We'd been through a long, dark valley, but now I was beginning to see the possibility that we could have a healthy marriage.

Chapter 61

January 2000

*M*y role as a pastor's wife began dreadfully.

Someone approached me in the church hallway one Sunday morning, shortly after Peter had begun his new position, and declared: "Perfect. I've wanted to talk to you about Bible study." She explained that they didn't have a women's Bible study and wanted to start one. And that I would be the one to lead.

"Why don't you ask someone else?" I asked. All the other ladies were older than me; surely one of them knew a lot about the Bible and would like to lead. What I meant, but didn't say out loud, was that I knew there was no way I could lead.

"Pastor's wife's job," she said. "At my old church, the pastor's wife always led the study." The lady who stood by her nodded in agreement. *What additional responsibilities are there,* I wondered. I had already complied with whatever expectations the church family had placed on me. After all, I had told Peter I would give him my full support.

Every night, I struggled through the Bible passages and questions in my study book as Peter patiently helped me. They were hard. Peter encouraged me to step down from leading, but my pride wouldn't let me. No way was I going to let the ladies know I was unintelligent or incapable.

Pride. Inferiority. Where did they come from? Actually, I knew the answer. Mom and Dad felt it themselves. Mom and Dad had never said I was stupid. Nor had they said I wasn't smart. Instead, Mom always compared her upbringing with mine, which led to guilt:

"You are lucky you always have a good time." Guilt.

"You are lucky you are allowed to sign in school." Guilt.

"You are lucky you don't have as many chores as I did." Guilt.

"You are lucky you get birthday and Christmas presents." Guilt.

And, "You are lucky you have a better education than we did." GUILT.

Guilt is a funny thing. For much of my early life, I worked hard to show Mom and Dad that I was not smarter than they were. But it was unavoidable. When they needed help or didn't understand something, they turned to me.

I felt at home among Mom and Dad's circle of friends. But among my classmates, their parents, or my teachers, it was a different story. They, too, were Deaf, but from a different class. Most of the parents and teachers had attended Gallaudet and held college degrees. The level and depth of their conversations were not the same as mine, and they didn't look at me as special. In other words, my intelligence was a given, not unique.

The combination of my guilt for being smarter than Mom and Dad, and my inferiority among MSD teachers, parents, and classmates had me subconsciously stuck between wanting to learn and holding myself back. Lack of affirmation at home didn't help either.

When I first wrote *him* letters, he had said they were beautiful. Compliment. He had enjoyed reading them. Compliment. He also said I had an excellent grasp of the language. Compliment. Why he bothered to comment on my language, I'm not sure. Was it in reference to something I had written in my letter? Was it because I told him I had thrown away my drafts? Was it because he recognized my lack of self-confidence when I was a student of his?

Had I *totally* believed him? No, because I had struggled with the issue for many years afterward. Yet, a wee tiny seed of confidence was planted. The words of encouragement were what I needed, and I clung to them, wanting to believe they were true. My leading Bible study had watered that seed waiting to sprout. I discovered my gift of teaching – I was good at presenting information in a clear and understandable fashion. I was able to draw people into sharing their feelings and thoughts. I created an environment where all kinds of questions, no matter how trivial or seemingly stupid, were welcomed.

I also discovered that I had the gift of wisdom. Ladies of all ages sought advice about everything: nutrition, disciplining children, finances, and resolving marital issues. And quite often, I had answers that were both constructive and reassuring.

Looking back, I had worried more about appearing intelligent and comparing myself to others than allowing myself to learn. Now, however, so many of the questions and challenges presented to me seemed to be a matter of common sense. And when I didn't have any answer, that was okay, too. I was realizing that my intelligence was not tied to what I knew (or didn't know). Nor was it the basis for my self-worth – one less pretense in my life.

Chapter 62

2000 – 2005

O ver the next several years, God's Word had transformed me, slowly but surely.

My transformation parallels my experience watching television while growing up. During the 1970s, our family had enjoyed watching *The Love Boat, The Incredible Hulk, Charlie's Angels, Little House on the Prairie, The Six Million Dollar Man,* and other shows of that era. Then, in the early 1980s, our lives change dramatically. To the delight of the Deaf community, we could connect a decoder to our TV, and for the first time, read the dialogue through closed-captioning. Finally, we could enjoy shows in their context; we could understand everything that was happening. And, I immediately realized that I could never *ever* sit through a noncaptioned show again.

That was my experience when I discovered the Truth – God's Word. As I began to really understand it, I couldn't and didn't want to return to my old way of life. My utmost desire was now to seek His ways. I was fed up with all the lies that were my life. Truth was something I had never experienced growing up. In our house, there were no honest answers to simple questions. It was always a guessing game. I never knew exactly what went through Mom and Dad's minds. I never knew exactly how they felt. I never knew what pleased them.

With God, it was different. I had been overwhelmed with His agape love. I was loved for who I was. There were no ifs, ands, or buts. He loved me – flaws and all. In other words, there was nothing I could do to make Him love me more. And, His Word remained the same – yesterday, today, and tomorrow.

The words on the calligraphy gift we received for our wedding now made sense. The Bible does have answers for work, marriage, raising a family, and all our other experiences in life.

Although Peter and I had brought some baggage into our marriage, we were able to work through it. We found ourselves growing closer in all areas of our lives. The more we studied God's Word, the better we understood what it meant to love each other unconditionally, to honor and respect each other, to submit to one another selflessly, and to give without expecting anything in return. Every year, we'd tell each other that we could not imagine our marriage getting any better. But, in fact, it was.

Home was a safe place for me – the only place I could be totally myself. I could share my feelings and thoughts freely. I was confident in my role as a mother – parenting had come to me so naturally. I could act silly around my family without worrying about their reactions. I laughed easily. I teased often. Life at home was filled with joy.

Despite the difficult years I had endured, by God's grace, I was able to maintain a positive outlook on life. My laid-back personality was a blessing; I dealt with various situations calmly and effectively. Our house was filled with kids from our neighborhood. They came and went all day long. Being Deaf had its advantages. I didn't mind the loud noises the children made – laughing and screaming. I didn't mind the mess they created.

Outside home, however, my confidence wavered. I became easily tongue-tied around people I considered smarter, more well-known, or out-spoken than me. I felt uncomfortable in large groups of people. I also did not trust people easily. It took me a very long time to open up to those I came in contact with regularly. Though people commented on my radiant smile, easy-going personality, and ability to maintain composure under stress, no one really knew me.

There was no doubt that my transformation had taken place. I was filled with joy and peace I'd never known before. Things I largely overlooked in the past, telling white lies, avoiding resolving conflicts, listening to gossip, and reading books or watching TV with vulgar or sexually explicit content, were no longer tolerable. I relied on the Bible when teaching my children life lessons: the importance of forgiveness, showing compassion to others, and especially remaining pure until marriage.

Yet, two things remained unchanged. My past was still a secret. And, I still longed for genuine friendships.

Chapter 63

Summer 2005

"Are you okay?" Peter asked when he noticed how quiet I was. I was normally talkative around my family.

I shrugged my shoulders. "It's nothing new," I said.

"Friends?" Peter guessed.

I nodded, fighting back my tears.

"Come here," Peter said, his arms outstretched, receiving me as I fell into his arms. "I'm so sorry you're still hurting," Peter said, trying to comfort me. "Did something happen at church this morning?"

"Not really. I just don't understand why. There must be something about me. What's wrong with me?" This was not the first time we'd talked about this subject. I blurted out that I had seen a few ladies discussing plans to get together.

"There's nothing wrong with you," Peter said.

"That's easy for you to say. You're biased. If there's nothing wrong with me, then how come I don't have friends?"

"I don't know. I wish I had answers."

Having friends was a prayer I had petitioned for so long. I'd recognized the consequences of my sin. All of this had happened because of *him*. But it had been more than fifteen years. Why was I still suffering?

I knew I was likable. I had to be. I had close friends all through my years at MSD. But confidence is a funny thing – after Gallaudet, I had begun to wonder. Perhaps, there was something wrong with me. Perhaps, something about me was a turn-off. Perhaps, I was boring. Perhaps…

Why had God not answered my prayers? From the day I'd met Peter, he had been my besterest friend and my soul mate. But there were days I'd wished for a close female friend.

I had tearfully asked Bridgetta the same thing when we talked one summer. She had moved to California, but when she visited her family, she would find time in her busy schedule to see me. Our time together every year was precious, although short.

"There is nothing wrong with you," Bridgetta had said.

In the early years of my marriage, our children had been the focus of my life. Being a mother was a joy, and I loved being around my children. Home was where my heart was, and I didn't believe in overscheduling our children with extracurricular activities. Had I missed out on opportunities to develop friendships as a result? Maybe so.

As the years had progressed, there were social gatherings I'd often declined. When it came to hosting parties, ladies wanted the freebies they got for being the hostess. I didn't need the stuff they were selling, and I didn't want to spend money just for the sake of getting together. Excuses on my part? Maybe so.

As I became pastor's wife, I suppose I had friends in church. But unfortunately they contacted me only when they needed something – my help, opinion, or advice. Given my role, I also knew too much – struggles our members faced, sins they committed, and issues the church faced. I was careful never to reveal private information.

I'd had moments of hope, though. Through the years – graduate school, work, and church – several ladies had crossed my path. We would get together a few times, but a friendship would not blossom. Once, I had tearfully opened up to a pastor's wife who was the mother of someone I knew.

"It's hard," I had said. "If I'd befriended someone in our congregation, it would have shown favoritism. It would be impossible to be close to certain ladies without hurting someone else's feelings." This pastor's wife understood my dilemma. For this reason, she had developed her circle of friends *outside* her church family. She had encouraged me to talk to her daughter, but I declined. I didn't want her to feel sorry and befriend me out of pity. I wanted someone to like me for who I was and who had the desire to get to know me better.

All of this had once again reminded me of *him*. If not for what had happened, I believe I would have had friends outside church. But I recognized that I couldn't use my past as an excuse, not any longer. I'd had my share of opportunities, but I had always found myself being on guard – wanting to get close, but at the same time, keeping myself at a distance. I recognized that I'm not an easy person to get to know. I had always been a private person, yet I had kept close friends. What was different now?

Perhaps this is one of the reasons I love my women's Bible study group. Week after week, I am with "friends" for an hour and a half. Over the years I have shared a little about myself, yet the ladies never probed. Was it because they were not interested? Or was it because of how they viewed me – the pastor's wife?

I am grateful for so much in my life, and I can honestly say that I'm content. But once in a while, I'm reminded of what I lack. And it hurts.

God answers prayers in three ways: yes, no, or later.

Chapter 64

Spring 2006

*I*t is difficult for me to imagine myself engaging in a relationship with a married man. How could I have allowed it to happen? I had known it was wrong from the very beginning – so why did I allow it to continue for two and a half years?

As a pastor's wife, people have often come to me for advice and confided in me their secrets and struggles. It was nothing new to me. I had grown up helping Mom and Dad. I grew up listening. I grew up with secrets and was good at keeping them.

In one instance, a woman I'll call Irene, came to me one day after our church service.

"Do you have a few minutes?" she asked.

"Sure," I said. "Is everything okay?"

"Yeah. You know, I've been through a lot." She was a single mother.

I nodded, and asked about one of her children, specifically. This child was struggling academically, and I wanted to know how she was doing.

"Pretty good. Change in schools helped. So far, doing well. Grades are improving. She seems happier."

"That's good to know. You wanted to talk to me about something in particular?"

"Yes. I've been seeing someone and I need your advice," she said. Then, before she explained further, she added: "Just between the two of us, okay? No one knows yet since he's still married."

"He's married?" I looked at her dumbfounded. What was she thinking?

"He plans to leave her and is in the process of getting a divorce," she explained.

"But he's still married. He needs to work on his marriage. You know, your relationship is adulterous, and you need to get out of it," I said.

"I know some Christians might think it is wrong, but don't you see? I've never been this happy before. God has answered my prayers. I've been praying for a husband. My children need a father as well." She proceeded to tell me how their paths had crossed. "It is obviously God's plan."

I had once thought that God worked like that as well, or so I wanted to believe. Actually, I knew from the very beginning that my affair was very wrong. But after a while, I had convinced myself that, perhaps, it was God's plan for me to be with *him*.

He had said that he wished he hadn't married his wife.

"But you did. So, you must have loved her," I had said.

"If I had known what being in love feels like, I wouldn't have," he'd said. *"I would have waited."*

"Waited for me? For so long?" It was difficult for me to believe that. "When I was born, you were already out of college and working. I don't think you would have waited."

"My marriage was obviously a mistake. I know now for sure that I was never in love. I thought I was, but I was wrong. It's you I'm in love with!" he'd said.

It's a hard thing for me to fathom now, but I had started to believe that perhaps he was right. God had *not* intended for him to marry his wife. After all, everyone makes mistakes, I reasoned. What if it really was God's plan for us to be together? God wants the best for us, doesn't He?

It was so easy to confuse the truth when my emotions got in the way. And now I listened as Irene was rationalizing her emotions, despite knowing the truth. I looked at her and wished I could share my story. But I couldn't. I didn't want his name exposed, or my name either, I suppose. Yet, I felt I was cheating her somehow by not sharing.

If she knew that I, too, was once deceived by Satan's lies, then perhaps, she would be more willing to listen to what I had to say. After all, I'd been there. But, instead, all I could offer was God's Word; not that I didn't trust that His Word could make an impact.

The advice she was seeking from me was whether or not they should live together. "You don't understand," she said when I told her it wasn't a good idea. Despite my advice, she followed her heart, and in the end, their relationship didn't work out.

There's great danger in following our hearts and not testing what we believe. As God said through Isaiah 55:8-9: For My thoughts are not your thoughts, nor are your ways My ways. For as the heavens are higher than the earth, so are My ways higher than your ways...

God's commands are for our protection. We create rules for our children for the same reason – we want to protect them, lead them on the right path, and bless them with good things that come as result of obedience.

God ultimately knows what is best for us, and if we obey His commands, that's what we get, His best.

Chapter 65

Summer 2006

*Y*ou must have wanted it to happen. Otherwise, you wouldn't have said anything," Peter said gently during one of our many conversations about the affair.

I couldn't believe he would have thought such a thing. "I don't think so," I said. "You make it sound as if I wanted to engage in an affair."

"No. But you could have kept it to yourself," Peter said. "Many students have fantasized about teachers, yet they don't act on it."

"I suppose I could have remained silent," I said. "I shared with *him* because I felt guilty. I also think I wanted to be disciplined."

"Disciplined?"

I had craved discipline. When I saw my friends being disciplined, I envied them. It showed that their parents cared about them. It also demonstrated their parents' love. I'm not talking about corporal punishment. I'd had my share of it while growing up. Mom would whip our hands or butts with a belt. But as we got older, Mom would send us to our rooms instead.

What I needed, though, was verbal discipline – parents sitting down with me to explain why this or that wasn't a good idea, wasn't allowed, or couldn't be done. As odd as it may seem, I yearned to be scolded and told what to do. During my high school years, whenever I asked Mom and Dad for their opinions, their typical response was: "It's up to you." When I asked if I could do this or that, they responded with: "If you want to."

"With him," I told Peter, "he was like a father to me. I had relied on his guidance and insight when dealing with my feelings. I had shared with him my fantasy because I knew it was wrong. Perhaps I'd hoped he would've taken the time to sit down and tell me how disappointed he was with me. That was something I'd never experienced growing up."

"That makes sense."

"It happened more than fifteen years ago. I wish I'd kept a copy of my confession note," I said. "I don't remember exactly what I wrote or what went through my mind at the time."

I think my deep desire for guidance and discipline in my life explains why it had been so easy for me to accept God's teaching. God had fulfilled the fatherly role I so desperately needed. He had loved me for who I was; He created me after all. He'd forgiven my wrongdoings. He had given me a second chance. He'd guided me through His teachings – the blueprint for my life. And He'd also affirmed my worth, I was someone special.

Chapter 66

September 2008

*I*n all the years I've been married, I'd never seen *him* outside MSD or MSD-related functions, but I bumped into his wife once at Sam's Club. I was in the frozen food section when I pushed my cart, turning left at the end of an aisle, and she was in the next aisle, turning right. For a second, I had wondered if he was with her – a quick but casual glance around told me he wasn't. We chatted for several minutes. When we departed, I told her to tell him I said hello.

During the first several years of my marriage, when Peter and I went out to the mall, a restaurant, or any public place, I would look out for him. Not because I wanted to see him, but because I didn't want to be caught unaware should I bump into him. So, when we did run into each other one morning, I was caught off-guard. It'd been so long since I'd last seen him. We hugged, as Deaf people always do when greeting each other. Neither of us had much time to spare, so we managed to catch up with each other in just a few minutes: health, family, job.

Memories of him, and us, flooded my mind as they did every time I saw him. Certain scenes from our past would replay in my mind and wouldn't go away for weeks at a time. I had wanted to see how he was really doing. Was he moving on with his life? Finding him was not too difficult, thanks to Google. He had shared enough information during our visit for me to look in the right places. I surfed the Internet for the organization where he volunteered. From their staff directory,

I was able to figure out what his email address might be if he had been given one.

I asked Peter how he would feel if I contacted him. Although a bit hesitant, he said that he trusted my judgment. So, I clicked the Send button:

Good morning.

I'm not sure if I have the correct e-mail address; hopefully this goes through to you.

It was a nice surprise seeing you last week; you looked good. I left feeling a bit frustrated because I wanted to see how you've been doing. Would it be possible for us to meet to catch up? (I have talked this over with Peter and have his permission to contact you).

If, for whatever reasons, you feel uncomfortable with the idea, please say so. I'll understand. If you are okay with the idea, when would be a good day/time for you?

Deb

* * *

Hi Deb,

It was great seeing you also. I left feeling the same way, but with so many people around it makes it difficult to catch up. You looked very good also. Ummm, I am not sure what your schedule is with home schooling and all. The first available day I have is 9th. We could meet for lunch somewhere. As I told you, I do some volunteer work and I could take an extended lunch break. If that is a problem let me know and we can

figure something else out. Please give my best to Peter.
Looking forward to meeting you.

* * *

Great. I'm glad my e-mail went through.
Unfortunately, 9th isn't good for me. Peter is off on
Mondays, so I can get away easiest that day. So meet
on a Monday, perhaps? Hope you are having a good
day!

Deb

After several emails back and forth, we agreed on a date. I
asked if he would feel comfortable meeting in Peter's office at
the church. I figured there wouldn't be too many people around.

That is fine, not a problem. Where is his office?

* * *

Friday is all set. We'll meet in Peter's office. Meet at
8:30 a.m. or 9:00 a.m.? Will your getting away on
Friday create problems with your wife? Are you going
to tell her we'll meet? Just wondering.

Deb

* * *

Deb,

Friday is fine. 8:30 a.m. would be great. My wife does

not know. I did tell her that I bumped into you and others at the park last week.

* * *

I see. If anything changes, you know where to reach me. Have a good week.

Chapter 67

October 2008

A week after our meeting, I emailed him again.
Good morning.

Our week flew by and before I knew it, it's Friday. I
had spent some time thinking and debating whether I
should write. I wanted to thank you for your willing-
ness to meet me last week. The hour and half went by
quickly, and I wouldn't have minded staying a bit longer, but that was okay. I was basically happy to know
you seem to be doing well.

I have a favor to ask; I'm not sure if you are comfortable with the idea, but here it is. I would like to meet
you again. This time, I would like for us to talk about
what happened twenty-plus years ago. Over the years,
I have always wondered about several things, and I
would like to have answers.

Don't get me wrong; I have a good marriage, and
Peter treats me very well. It's just that from time to
time, I would go down memory lane, and those same
questions would come back. Only you can answer
those questions, and I need to have those answers in
order to better understand what happened and why it
happened.

Take your time this weekend and think it over. If
you prefer that we discuss over email rather than in

person, that will be OK. If you feel uncomfortable with the idea of bringing up our past, then I'll just have to honor your wish. If you are in the same situation as I am and have some questions you would like to have answered, then great.

Hope your day is going well. Have a blessed weekend.

Deb

* * *

Deb,

Thank you for your email, and I agree it was nice to sit and chat. Memory lane, well, that is a place I often live in. I have questions also. Yes, I would be willing to chat again. Hopefully, it will be better than it was twenty years ago at Wendy's on Florida Ave. What day/time would be best? We can try to work something out. Maybe, the 5th? I could meet you at Peter's office around 1:00 p.m. If that is not good we can pick another day.

* * *

The 5th will not work. We won't be able to meet in Peter's office. Let me check my calendar and get back to you. In the meantime, could you refresh my memory as to what happened at Wendy's? Just a brief explanation will do. Thanks.

Deb

After a few messages back and forth regarding a date to meet, we decided on the 15th. I was nervous about the whole thing and didn't want to wait until Peter got home to let him know of my plans. So, I emailed him:

> He is willing to talk, and said he also has questions for me. We are going to meet on the 15th (time not determined and more likely, in your office). Please continue to pray for him. I hope I'm doing the right thing. I love you, and as I think back on what happened, I feel blessed that God had put you in my path.

* * *

Hi Love,

I trust you to do what is right. If you believe there is value in talking about all that, then I support it. I don't feel threatened; I am just protective of who God has given me to love and care for (you!). Thanks for sharing, and while I have expressed discomfort in the past about all that, I always want to know what is on your heart and mind. I love you.

* * *

Thanks. You're the besterest.

Chapter 68

October 2008

*W*anting to make most of our meeting, I scribbled down several questions:

What was missing in your marriage?

Was I the only one?

Was waiting until the kids had left the house an excuse, or did you plan on leaving her?

You're still married. Have things gotten better?

Does she know?

I was seventeen. What were you thinking? Why did you take the risk?

God has forgiven me. Have you asked for His forgiveness?

I stole glances at the paper as I drove to the church, hoping I'd remember them all. I didn't want to place the list on the table while we talked.

"How could you have fallen out of love so quickly?" he asked me, referring to the summer I'd left him. "You had just arrived in Texas when you wrote me the letter."

My feelings hadn't disappeared. "I used Peter as an excuse to leave you," I said defensively.

I found myself adding: "Remember when we made love? I was hoping I'd get pregnant."

"That makes me feel good," he said. "Thank you for telling me that."

I wanted to kick myself. Why had I told him that? I knew why. I felt he was questioning my character. He had made me feel guilty for leaving him so abruptly.

"When you left, I had made a decision. I was going to leave her in July and ask you to marry me when you returned from Texas," he said.

I looked at him dumbstruck. He was going to leave her.

"But you are still married to her," I said.

"I love her," he said. All of a sudden, a sickening feeling built inside me. I was hoping he'd say this, but actually hearing it was a different story. What did all our relationship mean then? Before I could think further, he looked at me and said: "But, I'm not in love with *her*. I'm in love with *you*."

"I'm a different person from who you knew," I said. "I was a total mess back then."

"You were so mature," he said, "unlike other girls in your class, how you behaved and talked set you apart."

"But I was only seventeen," I reminded him.

"We would have made it work," he said. He named a friend of his who had left his wife for a younger woman. "You should see them. They are very happy."

I then realized that we both were living in completely different worlds. He was not able to recognize the sin we had engaged in.

God was mentioned in our conversation, but I couldn't remember how we got to the subject. He said he attended church sometimes. I had asked why and he said, "Because it makes me feel good."

I had actually thought we'd have a discussion like two mature adults. Perhaps he would share how his wife had nagged him, driving him into my arms. How he had desperately needed admiration and respect. How his wife had invested her time and energy in their children rather than finding time for him. How the attention I gave him through my letters and poems had made him feel on the top of the world; anything that would justify his adultery. But none of this came up.

"What happened at Wendy's? You didn't say in the email," I asked.

"You scared the hell out of me when you threatened to never speak to me ever again if I said or did something. I can't remember what, exactly," he said. "I can't describe the feeling, but I was so scared. That was why I gave you a lot of room over the years."

"I don't remember our conversation," I said. "In fact, I remember almost nothing about my first two years at Gallaudet."

Driving home, I pondered our conversation. I was hoping I'd have a better understanding of what had taken place years ago. But that wasn't the case. It was so difficult for me to see his way of thinking. If we had married, we might have made it work, but that did not make our relationship right. And, the fact that he was still in love with me couldn't escape me.

If he had admitted the sin of our adultery, I'd have felt a bit more settled. But since he didn't and he still had feelings for me, Satan pulled the guilt I had nailed to the cross down and threw it back in my face.

I was hoping we could move past our history and finally be friends. But it couldn't be done, not with his thinking and feelings. He had kept our meeting a secret from his wife, which seemed unnecessary. But now, I'd understood why.

He is still in bondage.

And I am free.

Two completely different worlds.

Chapter 69

Same day

"How did the meeting go? Are you okay?" Peter was concerned. I had met *him* earlier that day.

"You won't like what he said." I looked at Peter, unsure of his reaction. "He is still in love with me. After all those years, he is still in love with me. Can you believe it?"

"I don't blame him. It's impossible not to love you." He reached out for my hand. "How did that make you feel?"

"Awkward. I didn't expect that. It has been over twenty years," I said. "How could he still be in love with me? I told him I am a different person now. But I have to be honest: I was a bit relieved when he said that."

"Relieved? What do you mean?"

I paused before I answered. "That means I was the only one. He did not take advantage of me. Am I making sense?"

"I disagree. I still think he took advantage of you. You know how I feel about this," Peter said. That was something we had talked about in the past. It was difficult for me to accept that, perhaps, he was right. "But I think I can see your point of view."

Peter then asked: "If he had asked you to marry him the summer you were in Texas, would you have?"

"I don't know. It's you I love. It's hard to imagine what my life would have been like if I did," I said, being careful with my words. The last thing I wanted was to hurt Peter, yet we'd always cherished honesty in our relationship. "If he had asked that summer, I am not sure. It's scary because I think I might have said yes. I don't know. It's hard to say now."

"I don't remember if you told me before, but had you two ever talked about getting married?"

I nodded. "He had talked about leaving her. We'd have to wait a few years, he'd said. Whenever we talked about our future, he would remind me of our age differences."

"I'd be so old and you'd still be young. I won't be able to keep up with you," he'd teased me.

"You are not that old! Who knows, I may die before you anyway," I said.

"When I'm bedridden, you'll be stuck by my bedside taking care of me," he'd cautioned.

"I'll gladly do that."

"People would stare at us, you know," he'd remind me.

"I don't care. That's their problem, not mine."

"Our friends may sidestep us," he reasoned.

"We could move so far away to where no one knows us. What's more, we'll have each other," I said.

"You deserve a wedding. It would be your first."

"Weddings cost money. We can just elope and I'll be happy as long as I have you," I'd assured him.

Back then, I couldn't see beyond the deception of our relationship. I may have considered consequences of marriage, but I was naïve to think that they wouldn't have mattered. Now, I shuddered to think of what I would have caused: Divorce. Broken home. Fractured relationships with his children. Hurt that would take years to heal. Financial loss. A jeopardized career.

I also shuddered to think of what I would have missed: My personal growth through therapy. A normal life. My beautiful marriage. The joy of raising our children. My church family. And, most important of all, my personal relationship with Jesus Christ.

Chapter 70

November 2008

$\mathcal{I}$have always been known as a calm and stable person –
regardless of the circumstances – but this time, I had
cried out to the Lord in despair.

"Why? Why me?" I asked.

After I left *him,* I had been angry. Because of him, I had
missed out on my college life. I had fallen into depression. I
did not develop lasting friendships. I had also lived with guilt
for many years.

But I was not angry with God. How could I be? God had
nothing to do with my misery. It was my confession when I
was seventeen that had gotten me into this mess.

Now, a mother of five, happily married, and a mature
Christian, I was able to see the whole picture in a different
light. I recognized that the blame was not entirely mine. Our
feelings were mutual. I was reminded that he had fantasized
about kissing me three months before I had made my fantasy
known. Our affair probably would have happened sooner or
later despite my confession.

As I pondered all of this, I began to question God. I understood my role as a sinner. But, what about everything I had
learned regarding God and His Sovereignty? How could our
mighty God have allowed the affair to happen? He was the
one who had placed me into a home without verbal or physical affection and affirmation. He had burdened me with the
responsibility of helping Mom and Dad. Wasn't that enough
for a child to carry? Why didn't God intervene? He could have

sent the right person to help me work through my grief when David left me. Why did He allow *him* to cross my path?

God had said through Jeremiah: "For I know the plans I have for you – plans to prosper you and not to harm you, plans to give you hope and a future" (29:11).

All of this didn't make sense as I shouted to Him: "How could you?" "Why didn't you?" "Why me?" "Why?"

I had no definite answers. My emotional turmoil only lasted a short while though; probably because I believe and trust that God's ways surpass my understanding.

I had moved on with my life after I'd nailed his name to the cross. But there were days like today, when Satan unexpectedly caught me off guard with questions to which I had no answers.

Chapter 71

Several Days Later

I did not want to admit it, but perhaps Peter was right. He had said he didn't like the idea of my seeing *him*, but he trusted my judgment. Was I a fool to think we could have an honest conversation about what had taken place? Was I a fool to think we could finally be friends? Was I a fool to think I could share God's Word with him?

How could he still be in love with me? It had been over twenty years.

How could he still not think that what had happened was wrong?

As soon as I had the house to myself, I knew what I needed to do. I walked to the basement and opened the door to what had become our storage, the space under our stairs. What I was looking for was somewhere in the midst of all the stuff I had stored: Christmas decorations, wrapping paper, surplus school supplies, snow pants and gloves, along with the vacuum, and several Rubbermaid boxes.

I created a path, crawled into the tiny space toward the back, and pulled out a green Rubbermaid box. Dragging it across the floor to our family room, I opened the box to make sure it was the right one. It was.

I carried it upstairs, sat down on the floor, and opened the top lid, removing all the contents from my high school years – pictures, essays I had written, medals I had won, and notes my friends had secretly passed to me. I was looking for any memorabilia I may have saved associated with *him*. After ten minutes, I realized that I had thrown away all of it except for his letters from the first summer we had corresponded. After digging some more, I came across my journals, my printed TTY conversations, and a stack of papers, which were bound with a paper clip. I looked at the cover page: "What can I say!!!"

I paused, trying to remember. What was this? Then, turning the page, I realized it was from him. When did he give them to me? I looked at the dates; they were written up to a year after I had left him. Slowly, the memories came as I began reading them one by one. I could no longer hold back my emotions.

> *Shady places, without traces*
> *Lonely trails, without tales*
> *Sharing time, yours and mine*
> *Country lanes, time change*
> *Girl dreams, lady in jeans*

Lady. All of your letters were addressed to me in that special name. Growing up, I never had a nickname. How I had cherished that name.

> *We meet, with kisses sweet*
> *Holding hands, making plans*
> *Clouds above, serious love*
> *Life's fine yours not mine*
> *Girl dreams, Lady in jeans*

What an irony! In the beginning, your life was fine, not mine. And, my life was not fine – not at all – for a very long time.

> *Dying is easy, I would be gone*
> *Living is hard the pain goes on*
> *Why can't my life follow a plan?*
> *Why am I just a man?*

I've been there, if you remember. I've spoken of my desire to die.

Being together
You and I
I saw the feelings
Watched you cry

How could you watch me cry and not do anything about it?

Good times together
Is what we had
Made me happy
Made you sad

If you had recognized my sadness, why didn't you just let me go?

So much pleasure
Being with you then
Will it return
I wonder when

Do not count on my returning to you. It'll never happen. It was all so wrong to begin with.

I would change things if only I could
Kiss the bruises and heal the wounds
Has been a long time since June
Only days, but ages it seems
All too clear, wishing for a dream
Mistakes, I made so many because
You spoke so little but listened a lot
I talked so much and listened not

Change the past to make new feelings
Looking back to change the ways
Living the memories day by day
Being alone and going home
Is not the same as going home alone
Problems you had more than a few

You spoke so little but listened a lot
I talked so much and listened not

Problems, you said. Thanks a lot. Yes, I spoke so little. So little. If you had listened to everything I had written the first year, you would have seen that I needed help. Instead, you had become a problem of mine.

I have no future, dreams of my own
I live in the past, I live alone
I never knew the price I'd pay
You said
I love you and went away.

I never knew the price I'd pay, either. I'm so sorry for the pain I've caused. I'm truly so very sorry. I wept, trying to make sense of the whole thing.

Chapter 72

Spring 2010

$\mathscr{I}$ noticed two sticks of butter on our kitchen counter. Next to them were vanilla extract, baking soda, baking powder, brown sugar, two eggs, and all-purpose flour. Savannah, our oldest daughter, was looking in the freezer as I walked into the kitchen.

"Where are chocolate chips?" Savannah asked when she saw me. "I thought we had some. I saw the bag a few days ago."

"It should be there," I said. "If not, check the garage." With five children, the extra freezer in the garage had become a necessity.

After Savannah returned from the garage with a 72-ounce Nestle bag in her hand, I asked: "Are the cookies for us?"

"No. For Julian."

"Again? You just made him some brownies last week."

"I know," she smiled. "He loves my homemade goodies."

"Savannah," I said. "I know we've talked about this before but I must repeat myself. It isn't a good idea. You're giving him the wrong idea."

"Mom!" She looked at me in exasperation. "I've told you many times. He's my best friend." They were inseparable at the school. They ate lunch together. They were in one or two classes together. They even walked together in between classes. Every night at dinner time, his name would come up in her conversation: his not-so-good relationship with his dad, his athletic achievements, and how teachers kept on referring to him to Savannah's "other half," which she found hilarious.

"But he has a girlfriend," I reminded her. "Does she know you've been making him special treats? I doubt it. I imagine she wouldn't like that." His girlfriend was a student at a different high school.

Fast forward several months later...

Savannah came home from school and asked: "Could we please talk?" So, we sat down on her bed.

"Is everything okay?" I was concerned. She seemed agitated.

"Julian and his girlfriend broke up."

I didn't say anything, but knew what was coming. We had talked about it numerous times.

"You were right," Savannah admitted.

"What do you mean?" not wanting to assume.

"You were right about him. He has feelings for me," Savannah said. "I didn't mean it. I really didn't."

"So, he left his girlfriend for you?" I asked.

"They've been having problems for some time. It seems that Julian has been talking about me a lot and it bothers her," Savannah said. Then, she added: "Now, Julian tells me he loves me."

"How do you feel about him?" She had denied any feelings toward him in the past.

"I only like him as a friend."

"Are you sure there's nothing more?"

"I'm sure," Savannah nodded.

Julian was crushed when Savannah told him that her feelings were not mutual. Her rejection, unfortunately, put an end to their friendship.

Later that night, I told Peter: "What was Savannah thinking? It was so obvious. I just wish she would have taken my advice." I shook my head in frustration. "People often tell me how mature Savannah is for her age, but at times, she is so naïve."

I was almost the same age as Savannah when my relationship with the teacher started. I'd always considered myself a mature girl. And, in many ways I was. But today, I was reminded that, ultimately, I was also a typical teenager – as irrational and naïve as any.

Chapter 73

April 2012

No!

Not long ago I had read headline that Jordan Powers, eighteen, had told Christopher James Hooker, forty-one, that she was done with him.

"Yes." I pumped my fist. Done. I knew it was not an easy thing to do, and I commended her strength to walk away.

Every time teacher–student scandals appeared in the news, they never failed to capture my attention. I couldn't fully relate to the affairs between teenagers sixteen and under and teachers in their twenties. But this one in particular was close to home. A teacher in his forties was married and had children. The only difference between this story and mine were that Hooker had left his wife for Powers, and they had appeared in public without shame. I had followed this story closely.

I could feel Powers' pain when she shared during her interview with ABC that she had "lost everything for this guy." Yet, now, she could start rebuilding her life.

But today, the headline read: "Modesto student moves back in with teacher arrested on sex charge."

No!

So many questions raced through my mind, as they always did:

How did their affair begin?

What was really happening in her life?

Surely, her parents must have suspected something was going on?

How could he have crossed his boundary as a trusted professional working with children?

I didn't believe that they had waited until she turned eighteen before their relationship turned physical. After our kiss, it had taken *him* only two weeks. I had resisted David's attempts to touch me. But with him, I didn't. I just couldn't.

It was one of a few scenes I remember vividly. We were alone in the building on campus when it happened. He had offered to take me home after school so that we could talk. He had taken me to a small room adjacent to the classroom, closed the door behind him, and began undressing me. He did not ask if it was okay. I wasn't even sure what he was doing. I didn't have time to react. I was scared. I knew we were alone in the building.

I could clearly see Powers as a victim.

There was no question that Hooker (ironically, the name was very fitting) exploited Powers (whose power didn't grant her enough strength to say "no"). What they had was not love, but his lust and power. Powers had mixed up love for affection and attention. Boundaries were clearly violated. He was an adult and she was a kid.

But, was I a victim? I had never looked at myself that way. It had never crossed my mind. Not even once.

Never mind the teacher's boundary. Never mind the teacher's age. Never mind the teacher's authority. Never mind the teacher's failure to protect me as a student. Never mind the teacher's...

Remember: I was the one who had started it.

Never mind that *his* letters the first summer contained inappropriate comments. Never mind that he had called me while vacationing with his family during the February break, a week before I had delivered him the note. Never mind that...

Remember: I was the one who had written the confession note.

I had asked Peter's colleague, a professional counselor, to read my story to get her perspective. Imagine my initial reaction, disbelief and denial, when she told me candidly that I was sexually exploited.

I didn't like what she had said.

And what may seem obvious to others was not apparent to me: She also said that what had happened to me almost thirty years ago was *not my fault.*

I was not responsible for the affair...I mean, the abuse.

I had thought I was past all the pain. But, once again, my world turned upside down. After several days of sorting through my feelings, I knew what Peter's colleague said was true. Every little thing I had pondered over the years now made sense. And, I thanked the Lord for this revelation. The very last burden I'd held on to for so long was finally lifted.

Yes. He was an adult.

And I was a kid.

About the Author

The daughter of Deaf parents, Deb Myers grew up in Williamsport, Maryland. She currently works as an adjunct professor, teaching American Sign Language, at two area colleges. Deb holds a master's degree in mental health counseling from Gallaudet University and has worked as a therapist serving Deaf teenagers and adults, in addition to working for a statewide early intervention program for Deaf children and their families. As a pastor's wife, she has served her Deaf congregation for the past 14 years, teaching, counseling, and leading marriage enrichment weekends. Deb has been married for 24 years and is the mother of five children—two of whom are adopted.

Deb has a passion for helping people discover wholeness and healing in their relationships through the power of forgiveness and redemption. *Deception* is her first book.

You may reach Deb at debmyersauthor@gmail.com

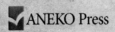

CPSIA information can be obtained at www.ICGtesting.com
Printed in the USA
BVOW04s2155090414

350256BV00009B/89/P